THE SONNETS OF MICHAEL ANGELO BUONARROTI AND TOMMASO CAMPANELLA

BY MICHAEL ANGELO BUONARROTI AND TOMMASO CAMPANELLA

TRANSLATED BY
JOHN ADDINGTON SYMONDS

PREFATORY NOTE.

After some deliberation, and at the risk of offending the sensibility of scholars, I have adopted the old English spelling of Michael Angelo's name, feeling that no orthographical accuracy can outweigh the associations implied in that familiar title. Michael Angelo has a place among the highest with Homer and Titian, with Virgil and Petrarch, with Raphael and Paul; nor do I imagine that any alteration for the better would be effected by substituting for these time-honoured names Homêros and Tiziano, Vergilius and Petrarca, Raffaello and Paulus.

I wish here to express my heartiest thanks to Signore Pasquale Villari for valuable assistance kindly rendered in the interpretation of some difficult passages of Campanella, and to Signore V. de Tivoli for calling my attention to the sonnet of Michael Angelo deciphered by him on the back of a drawing in the Taylor Gallery at Oxford.

Portions both of the Introduction and the Translations forming this volume, have already appeared in the 'Contemporary Review' and the 'Cornhill Magazine.'

DAVOS PLATZ:

Dec. 1877.

INTRODUCTION.

I.

It is with diffidence that I offer a translation of Michael Angelo's sonnets, for the first time completely rendered into English rhyme, and that I venture on a version of Campanella's philosophical poems. My excuse, if I can plead any for so bold an attempt, may be found in this—that, so far as I am aware, no other English writer has dealt with Michael Angelo's verses since the publication of his autograph; while Campanella's sonnets have hitherto been almost utterly unknown.

Something must be said to justify the issue of poems so dissimilar in a single volume. Michael Angelo and Campanella represent widely sundered, though almost contemporaneous, moments in the evolution of the Italian genius. Michael Angelo was essentially an artist, living in the prime of the Renaissance. Campanella was a philosopher, born when the Counter-Reformation was doing all it could to blight the free thought of the sixteenth century; and when the modern spirit of exact enquiry, in a few philosophical martyrs, was opening a new stage for European science. The one devoted all his mental energies to the realisation of beauty: the other strove to ascertain truth. The one clung to Ficino's dream of Platonising Christianity: the other constructed for himself a new theology, founded on the conception of God immanent in nature. Michael Angelo expressed the aspirations of a solitary life dedicated to the service of art, at a time when art received the suffrage and the admiration of all Italy. Campanella gave utterance to a spirit, exiled and isolated, misunderstood by those with whom he lived, at a moment when philosophy was hunted down as heresy and imprisoned as treason to the public weal.

The marks of this difference in the external and internal circumstances of the two poets might be multiplied indefinitely. Yet they had much in common. Both stood above their age, and in a sense aloof from it. Both approached poetry in the spirit of thinkers bent upon extricating themselves from the trivialities of contemporary literature. The sonnets of both alike are contributions to philosophical poetry in an age when the Italians had lost their ancient manliness and energy. Both were united by the ties of study and affection to the greatest singer of their nation, Dante, at a time when Petrarch, thrice diluted and emasculated, was the Phoebus of academies and coteries.

This common antagonism to the degenerate genius of Italian literature is the link which binds Michael Angelo, the veteran giant of the Renaissance, to Campanella, the audacious Titan of the modern age.

II.

My translation of Michael Angelo's sonnets has been made from Signor Cesare Guasti's edition of the autograph, first given to the world in 1863.[1] This masterpiece of laborious and minute scholarship is based upon a collation of the various manuscripts preserved in the Casa Buonarroti at Florence with the Vatican and other Codices. It adheres to the original orthography of Michael Angelo, and omits no fragment of his indubitable compositions.[2] Signor Guasti prefaces the text he has so carefully prepared, with a discourse upon the poetry of Michael Angelo and a description of the manuscripts. To the poems themselves he adds a prose paraphrase, and prints upon the same page with each composition the version published by Michelangelo Buonarroti in 1623.[3]

Before the publication of this volume, all studies of Michael Angelo's poetry, all translations made of it, and all hypotheses deduced from the sculptor's verse in explanation of his theory or his practice as an artist, were based upon the edition of 1623. It will not be superfluous to describe what that edition was, and how its text differed from that now given to the light, in order that the relation of my own English version to those which have preceded it may be rightly understood.[4]

Michael Angelo seems to have entertained no thought of printing his poems in his lifetime. He distributed them freely among his friends, of whom Sebastiano del Piombo, Luigi del Riccio, Donato Giannotti, Vittoria Colonna, and Tommaso de' Cavalieri were in this respect the most favoured. In course of time some of these friends, partly by the gift of the originals, and partly by obtaining copies, formed more or less complete collections; and it undoubtedly occurred to more than one to publish them. Ascanio Condivi, at the close of his biography, makes this announcement: 'I hope ere long to make public some of his sonnets and madrigals, which I have been long collecting, both from himself and others who possessed them, with a view to proving to the world the force of his inventive genius and the beauty of the thoughts produced by that divine spirit.' Condivi's promise was not fulfilled. With the exception of two or three pieces printed by Vasari, and the extracts quoted by Varchi in his 'Lezione,'[5] the poems of Michael Angelo remained in manuscript for fifty-nine years after his death. The most voluminous collection formed part of the Buonarroti archives; but a large quantity preserved by Luigi del Riccio, and from him transferred to Fulvio Orsini, had passed into the Vatican Library, when Michelangelo the younger conceived the plan of publishing his granduncle's poetry. Michelangelo obtained leave to transcribe the Vatican MSS. with his own hand; and after taking pains to collate all the autographs and copies in existence, he set himself to compare their readings, and to form a final text for publication. Here, however, began what we may call the Tragedy of his Rifacimento. The more he studied his great ancestor's verses, the less he liked or dared to edit them unaltered. Some of them expressed thoughts and sentiments offensive to the Church. In some the Florentine patriot spoke over-boldly. Others exposed their author to misconstruction on the score of personal morality.[6] All were ungrammatical, rude in versification, crabbed and obscure in thought—the rough-hewn blockings-out of poems rather than finished works of art, as it appeared to the scrupulous, decorous, elegant, and timorous Academician of a feebler age. While pondering these difficulties, and comparing the readings of his many manuscripts, the thought occurred to Michelangelo that, between leaving the poems unpublished and printing them in all their rugged boldness, lay the middle course of reducing them to smoothness of diction, lucidity of meaning, and propriety of sentiment.[7] In other words, he began, as Signer Guasti pithily describes his method, 'to change halves of lines, whole verses, ideas: if he found a fragment, he completed it: if brevity involved the thought in obscurity, he amplified: if the obscurity seemed incurable, he amputated: for superabundant wealth of conception he substituted vacuity; smoothed asperities; softened salient lights.' The result was that a medley of garbled phrases, additions, alterations, and sophistications was foisted on the world as the veritable product of the mighty sculptor's genius. That Michelangelo meant well to his illustrious ancestor is certain. That he took the greatest pains in executing his ungrateful and disastrous task is no less clear.[8] But the net result of his meddlesome benevolence has been that now for two centuries and a half the greatest genius of the Italian Renaissance has worn the ill-fitting disguise prepared for him by a literary 'breeches-maker.' In fact, Michael Angelo the poet suffered no less from his grandnephew than Michael Angelo the fresco painter from his follower Daniele da Volterra.

Nearly all Michael Angelo's sonnets express personal feelings, and by far the greater number of them were composed after his sixtieth year. To whom they were addressed, we only know in a few instances. Vittoria Colonna and Tommaso de' Cavalieri, the two most intimate friends of his old age in Rome, received from him some of the most pathetically beautiful of his love-poems. But to suppose that either the one or the other was the object of more than a few well-authenticated sonnets would be hazardous. Nothing is more clear than that Michael Angelo worshipped Beauty in the Platonic spirit, passing beyond its personal and specific manifestations to the universal and impersonal. This thought is repeated over and over again in his poetry; and if we bear in mind that he habitually regarded the loveliness of man or woman as a sign and symbol of eternal and immutable beauty, we shall feel it of less importance to discover who it was that prompted him to this or that poetic utterance. That the loves of his youth were not so tranquil as those of his old age, appears not only from the regrets expressed in his religious verses, but also from one or two of the rare sonnets referable to his manhood.

The love of beauty, the love of Florence, and the love of Christ, are the three main motives of his poetry. This is not the place to discuss at length the nature of his philosophy, his patriotism, or his religion; to enquire how far he retained the early teaching of Ficino and Savonarola; or to trace the influence of Dante and the Bible on his mind. I may, however, refer my readers who are interested in these questions, to the Discourse of Signor Guasti, the learned essay of Mr. J.E. Taylor, and the refined study of Mr. W.H. Pater. My own views will be found expressed in the third volume of my

'Renaissance in Italy'; and where I think it necessary, I shall take occasion to repeat them in the notes appended to my translation.

III.

Michael Angelo's madrigals and sonnets were eagerly sought for during his lifetime. They formed the themes of learned academical discourses, and won for him the poet's crown in death. Upon his tomb the Muse of Song was carved in company with Sculpture, Architecture, and Painting. Since the publication of the rifacimento in 1623, his verses have been used among the testi di lingua by Italians, and have been studied in the three great languages of Europe. The fate of Campanella's philosophical poems has been very different. It was owing to a fortunate chance that they survived their author; and until the year 1834 they were wholly and entirely unknown in Italy. The history of their preservation is so curious that I cannot refrain from giving some account of it, before proceeding to sketch so much of Campanella's life and doctrine as may be necessary for the understanding of his sonnets.

The poems were composed during Campanella's imprisonment at Naples; and from internal evidence there is good reason to suppose that the greater part of them were written at intervals in the first fourteen years of the twenty-five he passed in confinement.[9] In the descriptive catalogue of his own works, the philosopher mentions seven books of sonnets and canzoni, which he called 'Le Cantiche.'[10] Whether any of these would have been printed but for a mere accident is doubtful. A German gentleman, named Tobia Adami, who is supposed to have been a Court-Counsellor at Weimar, after travelling through Greece, Syria, and Palestine, in company with a young friend called Rodolph von Bunau, visited Campanella in his dungeon. A close intimacy sprang up between them, and Adami undertook to publish several works of the philosopher in testimony of his admiration. Among these were 'Le Cantiche.' Instead, however, of printing the poems in extenso, he made a selection, choosing those apparently which took his fancy, and which, in his opinion, threw most light on Campanella's philosophical theories. It is clear that he neglected the author's own arrangement, since there is no trace of the division into seven books. What proportion the selection bore to the whole bulk of the MS. seems to me uncertain, though the latest editor asserts that it formed only a seventh part.[11] The manuscript itself is lost, and Adami's edition of the specimens is all that now remains as basis for the text of Campanella's poems.

This first edition was badly printed in Germany on very bad paper, without the name of press or place. Besides the poems, it contained a brief prose commentary by the editor, the value of which is still very great, since we have the right to suppose that Adami's explanations embodied what he had received by word of mouth from Campanella. The little book bore this title:—'Scelta d' alcune poesie filosofiche di Settimontano Squilla cavate da' suo' libri detti La Cantica, con l'esposizione, stampato nell' anno MDCXXII.' The pseudonym Squilla is a pun upon Campanella's name, since both Campana and Squilla mean a bell; while Settimontano contains a quaint allusion to the fact that the philosopher's skull was remarkable for seven protuberances.[12] A very few copies of the unpretending little volume were printed; and none of these seem to have found their way into Italy, though it is possible that they had a certain circulation in Germany. At any rate there is reason to suppose that Leibnitz was not unacquainted with the poems, while Herder, in the Renaissance of German literature, published free translations from a few of the sonnets in his 'Adrastea.'

To this circumstance we owe the reprint of 1834, published at Lugano by John Gaspar Orelli, the celebrated Zurich scholar. Early in his youth Orelli was delighted with the German version made by Herder; and during his manhood, while residing as Protestant pastor at Bergamo, he used his utmost endeavours to procure a copy of the original. In his preface to the reprint he tells us that these efforts were wholly unsuccessful through a period of twenty-five years. He applied to all his literary friends, among whom he mentions the ardent Ugo Foscolo and the learned Mazzuchelli; but none of these could help him. He turned the pages of Crescimbeni, Quadrio, Gamba, Corniani, Tiraboschi, weighty with enormous erudition—and only those who make a special study of Italian know how little has escaped their scrutiny—but found no mention of Campanella as a poet. At last, after the lapse of a quarter of a century, he received the long-coveted little quarto volume from Wolfenbuttel in the north of Germany. The new edition which Orelli gave to the press at Lugano has this title:—'Poesie Filosofiche di Tommaso Campanella pubblicate per la prima volta in Italia da Gio. Gaspare Orelli, Professore all' Università di Zurigo. Lugano, 1834.' The same text has been again reprinted at Turin, in 1854, by Alessandro d'Ancona, together with some of Campanella's minor works and an essay on his life and writings. This third edition professes to have improved Orelli's punctuation and to have rectified his readings. But it still leaves much to be desired on the score of careful editorship. Neither Orelli nor D'Ancona has done much to clear up the difficulties of the poems—difficulties in many cases obviously due to misprints and errors of the first transcriber; while in one or two instances they allow patent blunders to pass uncorrected. In the sonnet entitled 'A Dio' (D'Ancona, vol. i. p. 102), for example, bocca stands for buca in a place where sense and rhyme alike demand the restitution of the right word.

At no time could the book have hoped for many readers. Least of all would it have found them among the Italians of the seventeenth and eighteenth centuries, to whom its energetic language and unfamiliar conceptions would have presented insuperable difficulties. Between Dante and Alfieri no Italian poet except Michael Angelo expressed so much deep thought and feeling in phrases so terse, and with originality of style so daring; and even Michael Angelo is monotonous in the range of his ideas and uniform in his diction, when compared with the indescribable violence and vigour of Campanella. Campanella borrows little by way of simile or illustration from the outer world, and he never falls into the commonplaces of poetic phraseology. His poems exhibit the exact opposite of the Petrarchistic or the Marinistic mannerism. Each sonnet seems to have been wrenched alive and palpitating from the poet's heart. There is no smoothness, no gradual unfolding of a theme, no rhetorical exposition, no fanciful embroidery, no sweetness of melodic cadence, in his masculine art of poetry. Brusque, rough, violent in transition, leaping from the sublime to the ridiculous—his poems owe their elevation to the intensity of their feeling, the nobleness and condensation of their thought, the energy and audacity of their expression, their brevity, sincerity, and weight of sentiment. Campanella had an essentially combative intellect. He was both a poet and a philosopher militant. He stood alone, making war upon the authority of Aristotle in science, of Machiavelli in state-craft, and of Petrarch in art, taking the fortresses of phrase by storm, and subduing the hardest material of philosophy to the tyranny of his rhymes. Plebeian saws, salient images, dry sentences of metaphysical speculation, logical summaries, and fiery tirades are hurled together— half crude and cindery scoriae, half molten metal and resplendent ore— from the volcano of his passionate mind. Such being the nature of Campanella's style, when in addition it is remembered that his text is sometimes hopelessly corrupt and his allusions obscure, the difficulties offered by his sonnets to the translator will be readily conceived.

IV.

At the end of the sixteenth and the beginning of the seventeenth centuries, philosophy took a new point of departure among the Italians, and all the fundamental ideas which have since formed the staple of modern European systems were anticipated by a few obscure thinkers. It is noticeable that the States of Naples, hitherto comparatively inert in the intellectual development of Italy, furnished the five writers who preceded Bacon, Leibnitz, Schelling, and Comte. Telesio of Cosenza, Bruno of Nola, Campanella of Stilo, Vanini and Vico of Naples are the chief among these novi homines or pioneers of modern thought. The characteristic point of this new philosophy was an unconditional return to Nature as the source of knowledge, combined with a belief in the intuitive forces of the human reason: so that from the first it showed two sides or faces to the world—the one positive, scientific, critical, and analytical; the other mystical, metaphysical, subjective. Modern materialism and modern idealism were both contained in the audacious guesses of Bruno and Campanella; nor had the time arrived for clearly separating the two strains of thought, or for attempting a systematic synthesis of knowledge under one or the other head.

The men who led this weighty intellectual movement burned with the passionate ardour of discoverers, the fiery enthusiasm of confessors. They stood alone, sustained but little by intercourse among themselves, and wholly misunderstood by the people round them. Italy, sunk in sloth, priest-ridden, tyrant-ridden, exhausted with the unparalleled activity of the Renaissance, besotted with the vices of slavery and slow corruption, had no ears for spirit-thrilling prophecy. The Church, terrified by the Reformation, when she chanced to hear those strange voices sounding through 'the blessed mutter of the mass,' burned the prophets. The State, represented by absolute Spain, if it listened to them at all, flung them into prison. To both Church and State there was peril in the new philosophy; for the new philosophy was the first birth-cry of the modern genius, with all the crudity and clearness, the brutality and uncompromising sincerity of youth. The Church feared Nature. The State feared the People. Nature and the People—those watchwords of modern Science and modern Liberty—were already on the lips of the philosophers.

It was a philosophy armed, errant, exiled; a philosophy in chains and solitary; at war with society, authority, opinion; self-sustained by the prescience of ultimate triumph, and invincible through the sheer force of passionate conviction. The men of whom I speak were conscious of Pariahdom, and eager to be martyred in the glorious cause. 'A very Proteus is the philosopher,' says Pomponazzo: 'seeking to penetrate the secrets of God, he is consumed with ceaseless cares; he forgets to thirst, to hunger, to sleep, to eat; he is derided of all men; he is held for a fool and irreligious person; he is persecuted by inquisitors; he becomes a gazing-stock to the common folk. These are the gains of the philosopher; these are his guerdon. Pomponazzo's words were prophetic. Of the five philosophers whom I mentioned, Vanini was burned as an atheist, Bruno was burned, and Campanella was imprisoned for a quarter of a century. Both Bruno and Campanella were

Dominican friars. Bruno was persecuted by the Church, and burned for heresy. Campanella was persecuted by both Church and State, and was imprisoned on the double charge of sedition and heresy. Dormitantium animarum excubitor was the self-given title of Bruno. Nunquam tacebo was the favourite motto of Campanella.

Giovanni Domenico Campanella was born in the year 1568 at Stilo in Calabria, one of the most southern townships of all Italy. In his boyhood he showed a remarkable faculty for acquiring and retaining knowledge, together with no small dialectical ability. His keen interest in philosophy and his admiration for the great Dominican doctors, Thomas Aquinas and Albertus Magnus, induced him at the age of fifteen to enter the order of S. Dominic, exchanging his secular name for Tommaso. But the old alliance between philosophy and orthodoxy, drawn up by scholasticism and approved by the mediaeval Church, had been succeeded by mutual hostility; and the youthful thinker found no favour in the cloister of Cosenza, where he now resided. The new philosophy taught by Telesio placed itself in direct antagonism to the pseudo-Aristotelian tenets of the theologians, and founded its own principles upon the Interrogation of Nature. Telesio, says Bacon, was the prince of the novi homines, or inaugurators of modern thought. It was natural that Campanella should be drawn towards this great man. But the superiors of his convent prevented his forming the acquaintance of Telesio; and though the two men dwelt in the same city of Cosenza, Campanella never knew the teacher he admired so passionately. Only when the old man died and his body was exposed in the church before burial, did the neophyte of his philosophy approach the bier, and pray beside it, and place poems upon the dead.

From this time forward Campanella became an object of suspicion to his brethren. They perceived that the fire of the new philosophy burned in his powerful nature with incalculable and explosive force. He moved restlessly from place to place, learning and discussing, drawing men towards him by the magnetism of a noble personality, and preaching his new gospel with perilous audacity. His papers were seized at Bologna; and at Rome the Holy Inquisition condemned him to perpetual incarceration on the ground that he derived his science from the devil, that he had written the book 'De tribus Impostoribus,' that he was a follower of Democritus, and that his opposition to Aristotle savoured of gross heresy. At the same time the Spanish Government of Naples accused him of having set on foot a dangerous conspiracy for overthrowing the vice-regal power and establishing a communistic commonwealth in southern Italy. Though nothing was proved satisfactorily against him, Campanella was held a prisoner under the sentence which the Inquisition had pronounced upon him. He was, in fact, a man too dangerous, too original in his opinions, and too bold in their enunciation, to be at large. For twenty-five years he remained in Neapolitan dungeons; three times during that period he was tortured to the verge of dying; and at last he was released, while quite an old man, at the urgent request of the French Court. Not many years after his liberation Campanella died. The numerous philosophical works on metaphysics, mathematics, politics, and aesthetics which Campanella gave to the press, were composed during his long imprisonment. How they came to be printed, I do not know; but it is obvious that he cannot have been strictly debarred from writing by his jailors. In prison, too, he made both friends and converts. We have seen that we owe the publication of a portion of his poems to the visit of a German knight.

V.

The sonnets by Campanella translated in this volume might be rearranged under four headings—Philosophical; Political; Prophetic; Personal. The philosophical group throw light on Campanella's relation to his predecessors and his antagonism to the pseudo-Aristotelian scholasticism of the middle ages. They furthermore explain his conception of the universe as a complex animated organism, his conviction that true knowledge can only be gained by the interrogation of nature, his doctrine of human life and action, and his judgment of the age in which he lived. The political sonnets fall into two groups— those which discuss royalty, nobility, and the sovereignty of the people, and those which treat of the several European states. The prophetic sonnets seem to have been suggested by the misery and corruption of Italy, and express the poet's belief in the speedy triumph of right and reason. It is here too that his astrological opinions are most clearly manifested; for Campanella was far from having outgrown the belief in planetary influences. Indeed, his own metaphysical speculations, involving the principle of immanent vitality in the material universe, gave a new value to the dreams of the astrologers. Among the personal sonnets may be placed those which refer immediately to his own sufferings in prison, to his friendships, and to the ideal of the philosophic character.

I have thought it best, while indicating this fourfold division, to preserve the order adopted by Adami, since each of the reprints accessible to modern readers—both that of Orelli and that of D'Ancona— maintains the arrangement of the editio princeps. Two sonnets of the prophetic group I have omitted, partly because they have no bearing on the world as it exists for us at present, and partly because they are too studiously obscure for profitable reproduction.[13] As in the case of Michael Angelo, so also in that of Campanella, I have left the Canzoni untouched, except by way of illustration in the notes appended to my volume. They are important and voluminous enough to form a separate book; nor do they seem to me so well adapted as the sonnets for translation into English.

To give reasons for my choice of certain readings in the case of either Michael Angelo's or Campanella's text; to explain why I have sometimes preferred a strictly literal and sometimes a more paraphrastic rendering; or to set forth my views in detail regarding the compromises which are necessary in translation, and which must vary according to the exigencies of each successive problem offered by the original, would occupy too much space. Where I have thought it absolutely necessary, I have referred to such points in my notes. It is enough here to remark that the difficulties presented to the translator by Michael Angelo and by Campanella are of different kinds. Both, indeed, pack their thoughts so closely that it is not easy to reproduce them without either awkwardness or sacrifice of matter. But while Campanella is difficult from the abruptness of his transitions and the violence of his phrases, Michael Angelo has the obscurity of a writer whose thoughts exceed his power of expression, and who complicates the verbal form by his endeavour to project what cannot easily be said in verse.[14] A little patience will generally make it clear what Campanella meant, except in cases where the text itself is corrupt. But it may sometimes be doubted whether Michael Angelo could himself have done more than indicate the general drift of his thought, or have disengaged his own conception from the tangled skein of elliptical and ungrammatical sentences in which he has enveloped it. The form of Campanella's poetry, though often grotesque, is always clear. Michael Angelo has left too many of his compositions in the same state as his marbles—unfinished and colossal abbozzi, which lack the final touches to make their outlines distinct. Under these circumstances, it can hardly happen that the translator should succeed in reproducing all the sharpness and vivacity of Campanella's style, or should wholly refrain from softening, simplifying, and prettifying Michael Angelo in his attempt to produce an intelligible version. In both cases he is tempted to make his translation serve the purpose also of a commentary, and has to exercise caution and self-control lest he impose a sense too narrow or too definite upon the original.

So far as this was possible, I have adhered to the rhyming structure of my originals, feeling that this is a point of no small moment in translation. Yet when the choice lay between a sacrifice of metrical exactitude and a sacrifice of sense, I have not hesitated to prefer the former, especially in dealing with Campanella's quatrains.

Michael Angelo and Campanella follow different rules in their treatment of the triplets. Michael Angelo allows himself three rhymes, while Campanella usually confines himself to two. My practice has been to study in each sonnet the cadence both of thought and diction, so as to satisfy an English ear, accustomed to the various forms of termination exemplified by Spenser, Milton, Wordsworth, and Rossetti—the sweetest, the most sublime, the least artificial, and the most artful sonnet-writers in our language.

The short titles attached to each sonnet are intended to help the eye, rather than to guide the understanding of the reader. Michael Angelo and his editors supply no arguments or mottoes for his poems; while those printed by Adami in his edition of Campanella are, like mine, meant obviously to serve as signposts to the student. It may savour of impudence to ticket and to label little masterpieces, each one of which, like all good poems, is a microcosm of very varied meanings. Yet I have some authority in modern times for this impertinence; and, when it is acknowledged that the titles merely profess to guide the reader through a labyrinth of abstract and reflective compositions, without attempting to supply him with a comprehensive argument or to dogmatise concerning the main drift of each poem, I trust that enough will have been said by way of self-defence against the charge of arrogance.

The sonnet prefixed as a proem to the whole book is generally attributed to Giordano Bruno, in whose Dialogue on the Eroici Furori it occurs. There seems, however, good reason to suppose that it was really written by Tansillo, who recites it in that Dialogue. Whoever may have been its author, it expresses in noble and impassioned verse the sense of danger, the audacity, and the exultation of those pioneers of modern thought, for whom philosophy was a voyage of discovery into untravelled regions. Its spirit is rather that of Campanella than of Michael Angelo. Yet the elevation at which Michael Angelo habitually lived in thought and feeling was so far above the plains of common life, that from the summit of his solitary watch-tower he might have followed even such high-fliers as Bruno or as Campanella in their Icarian excursions with the eyes of speculative interest.

DAVOS PLATZ. Nov. 1877.

FOOTNOTES

[1] 'Le Rime di Michelangelo Buonarroti, Pittore, Scultore e Architetto, cavate dagli Autografi e pubblicate da Cesare Guasti, Accademico della Crusca. In Firenze, per Felice le Monmer. MDCCCLXIII.'

[2] See, however, page xlvii of Signor Guasti's Discorso.

[3] I have so fully expressed my admiration for Signor Guasti's edition in the text that I may allow myself to point out in a note what seems to me its chief defect, and why I think there is still, perhaps, room for another and more critical edition. The materials are amply and conscientiously supplied by Signor Guasti, indeed, I suppose we are justified in believing that his single volume reproduces all the extant manuscript authorities, with the exception, perhaps, of the British Museum Codex. But, while it is so comprehensive, we are still left in some doubt as to the preference of one reading rather than another in the large type text presented to us as the final version of each composition. It is true that when this was possible, Signor Guasti invariably selected one of the autographs, that is, a copy in the poet's own handwriting. But when we consider that very frequently Michael Angelo's own autographs give twice as many various readings as there are lines in a sonnet, when we reflect that we do not always possess the copies which he finally addressed to his friends, and when, moreover, we find that their readings (e.g. those of the Riccio MS and those cited by Varchi) differ considerably from Michael Angelo's rough copies, we must conclude that even the autographs do not invariably represent these poems in the final form which he adopted. There is therefore much room left for critical comparison and selection. We are, in fact, still somewhat in the same position as Michelangelo the younger. Whether any application of the critical method will enable us to do again successfully what he so clumsily attempted—that is, to reproduce a correct text from the debris offered to our selective faculty—I do not feel sure. Meanwhile I am quite certain that his principle was a wrong one, and that he dealt most unjustifiably with his material. For this reason I cordially accept Signor Guasti's labours, with the reservation I have attempted to express in this note. They have indeed brought us far closer to Michael Angelo's real text, but we must be careful to remember that we have not even now arrived with certainty at what he would himself have printed if he had prepared his own edition for the press.

[4] As far as I am aware, no complete translation of Michael Angelo's sonnets has hitherto been made in English. The specimens produced by Southey, Wordsworth, Harford, Longfellow, and Mr. Taylor, moreover, render Michelangelo's rifacimento.

[5] 'Lezione di Benedetto Varchi sopra il sottoscritto Sonetto di Michelagnolo Buonarroti, fatta da lui pubblicamente nella Accademia Fiorentina la Seconda Domenica di Quaresima l'anno MDXLVI.' The sonnet commented by Varchi is Guasti's No xv.

[6] I have elsewhere recorded my disagreement with Signer Guasti and Signer Gotti, and my reasons for thinking that Vaichi and Michelangelo the younger were right in assuming that the sonnets addressed to Tommaso de' Cavalieri (especially xxx, xxxi, lii) expressed the poet's admiration for masculine beauty. See 'Renaissance in Italy, Fine Arts,' pp. 521, 522. At the same time, though I agree with Buonarroti's first editor in believing that a few of the sonnets 'risguardano, come si conosce chiaramente, amor platonico virile,' I quite admit—as what student of early Italian poetry will not admit?—that a woman is generally intended under the title of 'Signore' and 'amico.'

[7] Ridurle is his own phrase. He also speaks of trasmutare and risoluzione to explain the changes he effected.

[8] See Guasti's 'Discorso,' p. xliv.

[9] See in particular 'Orazioni Tie in Salmodia Metafisicale ... Canzone Prima ... Madrigale iii;' and 'A Berillo, Canzone di Pentimento, Madrigale ii.'

[10] 'De Libras Proprus,' I 3, quoted by Orelli and Alessandro d'Ancona. 'Opere di Tommaso Campanella,' vol. I. p 3.

[11] 'Opere di Tommaso Campanella,' vol. I p. ccci.

[12] Campanella's own poetry justified this curious nom de plume adopted for him by his editor. See in particular 'Salmodia Metafisicale,' canzone terza, madrigale ix.

'Tre canzon, nate a un parto
Da questa mia settimontana testa,
Al suon dolente di pensosa squilla.'

[13] These are the sonnets entitled by Adami 'La detta Congiunzione cade nella revoluzione della Natività di Cristo,' and 'Sonetto cavato dall' Apocalisse e Santa Brigida,' D'Ancona, vol. 1. pp. 97, 98.

[14] In this respect rifacimento of 1623 has greater literary merits— the merits of mere smoothness, clearness, grammatical coherence, and intelligibility—than the autograph; and I can understand the preference of some students for the former, though I do not share it Michelangelo the younger added fluency and grace to his great-uncle's composition by the sacrifice of much that is most characteristic, and by the omission of much that is profound and vigorous and weighty.

PROEM.

THE PHILOSOPHIC FLIGHT.

Poi che spiegate.

Now that these wings to speed my wish ascend,
  The more I feel vast air beneath my feet,
  The more toward boundless air on pinions fleet,
  Spurning the earth, soaring to heaven, I tend:
Nor makes them stoop their flight the direful end
  Of Daedal's son; but upward still they beat:—
  What life the while with my life can compete,
  Though dead to earth at last I shall descend?
My own heart's voice in the void air I hear:
  Where wilt thou bear me, O rash man? Recall
  Thy daring will! This boldness waits on fear!
Dread not, I answer, that tremendous fall:

Strike through the clouds, and smile when death is near,
If death so glorious be our doom at all!

THE SONNETS

OF

MICHAEL ANGELO BUONARROTI

I.

ON DANTE ALIGHIERI.

Dal ciel discese.

From heaven his spirit came, and robed in clay
The realms of justice and of mercy trod,
Then rose a living man to gaze on God,
That he might make the truth as clear as day.
For that pure star that brightened with his ray
The undeserving nest where I was born,
The whole wide world would be a prize to scorn;
None but his Maker can due guerdon pay.
I speak of Dante, whose high work remains
Unknown, unhonoured by that thankless brood,
Who only to just men deny their wage.
Were I but he! Born for like lingering pains,
Against his exile coupled with his good
I'd gladly change the world's best heritage!

II.

ON DANTE ALIGHIERI.

Quante dirne si de'.

No tongue can tell of him what should be told,
For on blind eyes his splendour shines too strong;
'Twere easier to blame those who wrought him wrong,
Than sound his least praise with a mouth of gold.
He to explore the place of pain was bold,
Then soared to God, to teach our souls by song;
The gates heaven oped to bear his feet along,
Against his just desire his country rolled.
Thankless I call her, and to her own pain
The nurse of fell mischance; for sign take this,
That ever to the best she deals more scorn:
Among a thousand proofs let one remain;
Though ne'er was fortune more unjust than his,
His equal or his better ne'er was born.

III.

TO POPE JULIUS II.

Signor, se vero è.

My Lord! if ever ancient saw spake sooth,
Hear this which saith: Who can, doth never will.
Lo! thou hast lent thine ear to fables still,
Rewarding those who hate the name of truth.
I am thy drudge and have been from my youth—
Thine, like the rays which the sun's circle fill;
Yet of my dear time's waste thou think'st no ill:
The more I toil, the less I move thy ruth.
Once 'twas my hope to raise me by thy height;
But 'tis the balance and the powerful sword
Of Justice, not false Echo, that we need.
Heaven, as it seems, plants virtue in despite
Here on the earth, if this be our reward—
To seek for fruit on trees too dry to breed.
IV.

ON ROME IN THE PONTIFICATE OF JULIUS II.

Qua si fa elmi.

Here helms and swords are made of chalices:
The blood of Christ is sold so much the quart:
His cross and thorns are spears and shields; and short
Must be the time ere even his patience cease.
Nay let him come no more to raise the fees
Of this foul sacrilege beyond report!
For Rome still flays and sells him at the court,
Where paths are closed to virtue's fair increase.
Now were fit time for me to scrape a treasure!
Seeing that work and gain are gone; while he
Who wears the robe, is my Medusa still.
God welcomes poverty perchance with pleasure:
But of that better life what hope have we,
When the blessed banner leads to nought but ill?
V.

TO GIOVANNI DA PISTOJA.

ON THE PAINTING OF THE SISTINE CHAPEL.

I' ho già fatto un gozzo.

I've grown a goitre by dwelling in this den—
As cats from stagnant streams in Lombardy,

Or in what other land they hap to be—
Which drives the belly close beneath the chin:
My beard turns up to heaven; my nape falls in,
Fixed on my spine: my breast-bone visibly
Grows like a harp: a rich embroidery
Bedews my face from brush-drops thick and thin.
My loins into my paunch like levers grind:
My buttock like a crupper bears my weight;
My feet unguided wander to and fro;
In front my skin grows loose and long; behind,
By bending it becomes more taut and strait;
Crosswise I strain me like a Syrian bow:
Whence false and quaint, I know,
Must be the fruit of squinting brain and eye;
For ill can aim the gun that bends awry.
Come then, Giovanni, try
To succour my dead pictures and my fame;
Since foul I fare and painting is my shame.
VI.

INVECTIVE AGAINST THE PEOPLE OF PISTOJA.

I' l' ho, vostra mercè.

I've gotten it, thanks to your courtesy;
And I have read it twenty times or so:
Thus much may your sharp snarling profit you,
As food our flesh filled to satiety.
After I left you, I could plainly see
How Cain was of your ancestors: I know
You do not shame his lineage, for lo,
Your brother's good still seems your injury.
Envious you are, and proud, and foes to heaven;
Love of your neighbour still you loathe and hate,
And only seek what must your ruin be.
If to Pistoja Dante's curse was given,
Bear that in mind! Enough! But if you prate
Praises of Florence, 'tis to wheedle me.
A priceless jewel she:
Doubtless: but this you cannot understand:
For pigmy virtue grasps not aught so grand.
VII.

TO LUIGI DEL RICCIO.

Nel dolce d' una.

It happens that the sweet unfathomed sea
Of seeming courtesy sometimes doth hide

Offence to life and honour. This descried,
I hold less dear the health restored to me.
He who lends wings of hope, while secretly
He spreads a traitorous snare by the wayside,
Hath dulled the flame of love, and mortified
Friendship where friendship burns most fervently.
Keep then, my dear Luigi, clear and pure
That ancient love to which my life I owe,
That neither wind nor storm its calm may mar.
For wrath and pain our gratitude obscure;
And if the truest truth of love I know,
One pang outweighs a thousand pleasures far.

VIII.

TO LUIGI DEL RICCIO,

AFTER THE DEATH OF CECCHINO BRACCI.

A pena prima.

Scarce had I seen for the first time his eyes
Which to your living eyes were life and light,
When closed at last in death's injurious night
He opened them on God in Paradise.
I know it and I weep, too late made wise:
Yet was the fault not mine; for death's fell spite
Robbed my desire of that supreme delight,
Which in your better memory never dies.
Therefore, Luigi, if the task be mine
To make unique Cecchino smile in stone
For ever, now that earth hath made him dim,
If the beloved within the lover shine,
Since art without him cannot work alone,
You must I carve to tell the world of him.

IX.

THANKS FOR A GIFT.

Al zucchero, alla mula.

The sugar, candles, and the saddled mule,
Together with your cask of malvoisie,
So far exceed all my necessity
That Michael and not I my debt must rule,
In such a glassy calm the breezes fool
My sinking sails, so that amid the sea
My bark hath missed her way, and seems to be
A wisp of straw whirled on a weltering pool.
To yield thee gift for gift and grace for grace,

For food and drink and carriage to and fro,
For all my need in every time and place,
O my dear lord, matched with the much I owe,
All that I am were no real recompense:
Paying a debt is not munificence.

X.

TO GANDOLFO PORRINO.

ON HIS MISTRESS FAUSTINA MANCINA.

La nuova alta beltà.

That new transcendent fair who seems to be
Peerless in heaven as in this world of woe,
(The common folk, too blind her worth to know
And worship, called her Left Arm wantonly),
Was made, full well I know, for only thee:
Nor could I carve or paint the glorious show
Of that fair face: to life thou needs must go,
To gain the favour thou dost crave of me.
If like the sun each star of heaven outshining,
She conquers and outsoars our soaring thought,
This bids thee rate her worth at its real price.
Therefore to satisfy thy ceaseless pining,
Once more in heaven hath God her beauty wrought:
God and not I can people Paradise.

XI.

TO GIORGIO VASARI.

ON THE LIVES OF THE PAINTERS.

Se con lo stile.

With pencil and with palette hitherto
You made your art high Nature's paragon;
Nay more, from Nature her own prize you won,
Making what she made fair more fair to view.
Now that your learnéd hand with labour new
Of pen and ink a worthier work hath done,
What erst you lacked, what still remained her own,
The power of giving life, is gained for you.
If men in any age with Nature vied
In beauteous workmanship, they had to yield
When to the fated end years brought their name.
You, reilluming memories that died,
In spite of Time and Nature have revealed
For them and for yourself eternal fame.

XII.

TO VITTORIA COLONNA.

A MATCHLESS COURTESY.

Felice spirto.

Blest spirit, who with loving tenderness
   Quickenest my heart so old and near to die,
   Who mid thy joys on me dost bend an eye
   Though many nobler men around thee press!
As thou wert erewhile wont my sight to bless,
   So to console my mind thou now dost fly;
   Hope therefore stills the pangs of memory,
   Which coupled with desire my soul distress.
So finding in thee grace to plead for me—
   Thy thoughts for me sunk in so sad a case—
   He who now writes, returns thee thanks for these.
Lo, it were foul and monstrous usury
   To send thee ugliest paintings in the place
   Of thy fair spirit's living phantasies.
XIII.

TO VITTORIA COLONNA.

BRAZEN GIFTS FOR GOLDEN.

Per esser manco almen.

Seeking at least to be not all unfit
   For thy sublime and boundless courtesy,
   My lowly thoughts at first were fain to try
   What they could yield for grace so infinite.
But now I know my unassisted wit
   Is all too weak to make me soar so high;
   For pardon, lady, for this fault I cry,
   And wiser still I grow remembering it.
Yea, well I see what folly 'twere to think
   That largess dropped from thee like dews from heaven
   Could e'er be paid by work so frail as mine!
To nothingness my art and talent sink;
   He fails who from his mortal stores hath given
   A thousandfold to match one gift divine.
XIV.

FIRST READING.

TO VITTORIA COLONNA.

THE MODEL AND THE STATUE.

Da che concetto.

When divine Art conceives a form and face,
   She bids the craftsman for his first essay
   To shape a simple model in mere clay:
   This is the earliest birth of Art's embrace.
From the live marble in the second place
   His mallet brings into the light of day
   A thing so beautiful that who can say
   When time shall conquer that immortal grace?
Thus my own model I was born to be—
   The model of that nobler self, whereto
   Schooled by your pity, lady, I shall grow.
Each overplus and each deficiency
   You will make good. What penance then is due
   For my fierce heat, chastened and taught by you?
XIV.

SECOND READING.

To VITTORIA COLONNA.

THE MODEL AND THE STATUE.

Se ben concetto.

When that which is divine in us doth try
   To shape a face, both brain and hand unite
   To give, from a mere model frail and slight,
   Life to the stone by Art's free energy.
Thus too before the painter dares to ply
   Paint-brush or canvas, he is wont to write
   Sketches on scraps of paper, and invite
   Wise minds to judge his figured history.
So, born a model rude and mean to be
   Of my poor self, I gain a nobler birth,
   Lady, from you, you fountain of all worth!
Each overplus and each deficiency
   You will make good. What penance then is due
   For my fierce heat, chastened and taught by you?
XV.

THE LOVER AND THE SCULPTOR.

Non ha l' ottimo artista.

The best of artists hath no thought to show
Which the rough stone in its superfluous shell
Doth not include: to break the marble spell
Is all the hand that serves the brain can do.
The ill I shun, the good I seek, even so
In thee, fair lady, proud, ineffable,
Lies hidden: but the art I wield so well
Works adverse to my wish, and lays me low.
Therefore not love, nor thy transcendent face,
Nor cruelty, nor fortune, nor disdain,
Cause my mischance, nor fate, nor destiny;
Since in thy heart thou carriest death and grace
Enclosed together, and my worthless brain
Can draw forth only death to feed on me.

XVI.

LOVE AND ART.

Sì come nella penna.

As pen and ink alike serve him who sings
In high or low or intermediate style;
As the same stone hath shapes both rich and vile
To match the fancies that each master brings;
So, my loved lord, within thy bosom springs
Pride mixed with meekness and kind thoughts that smile:
Whence I draw nought, my sad self to beguile,
But what my face shows—dark imaginings.
He who for seed sows sorrow, tears, and sighs,
(The dews that fall from heaven, though pure and clear,
From different germs take divers qualities)
Must needs reap grief and garner weeping eyes;
And he who looks on beauty with sad cheer,
Gains doubtful hope and certain miseries.

XVII.

THE ARTIST AND HIS WORK.

Com' esser, donna, può.

How can that be, lady, which all men learn
By long experience? Shapes that seem alive,
Wrought in hard mountain marble, will survive
Their maker, whom the years to dust return!
Thus to effect cause yields. Art hath her turn,
And triumphs over Nature. I, who strive
With Sculpture, know this well; her wonders live
In spite of time and death, those tyrants stern.
So I can give long life to both of us

In either way, by colour or by stone,
Making the semblance of thy face and mine.
Centuries hence when both are buried, thus
Thy beauty and my sadness shall be shown,
And men shall say, 'For her 'twas wise to pine.'
XVIII.

BEAUTY AND THE ARTIST.

Al cor di zolfo.

A heart of flaming sulphur, flesh of tow,
Bones of dry wood, a soul without a guide
To curb the fiery will, the ruffling pride
Of fierce desires that from the passions flow;
A sightless mind that weak and lame doth go
Mid snares and pitfalls scattered far and wide;—
What wonder if the first chance brand applied
To fuel massed like this should make it glow?
Add beauteous art, which, brought with us from heaven,
Will conquer nature;—so divine a power
Belongs to him who strives with every nerve.
If I was made for art, from childhood given
A prey for burning beauty to devour,
I blame the mistress I was born to serve.
XIX.

THE AMULET OF LOVE.

Io mi son caro assai più.

Far more than I was wont myself I prize:
With you within my heart I rise in rate,
Just as a gem engraved with delicate
Devices o'er the uncut stone doth rise;
Or as a painted sheet exceeds in price
Each leaf left pure and in its virgin state:
Such then am I since I was consecrate
To be the mark for arrows from your eyes.
Stamped with your seal I'm safe where'er I go,
Like one who carries charms or coat of mail
Against all dangers that his life assail
Nor fire nor water now may work me woe;
Sight to the blind I can restore by you,
Heal every wound, and every loss renew.
XX.

THE GARLAND AND THE GIRDLE.

Quanta si gode, lieta.

What joy hath yon glad wreath of flowers that is
   Around her golden hair so deftly twined,
   Each blossom pressing forward from behind,
   As though to be the first her brows to kiss!
The livelong day her dress hath perfect bliss,
   That now reveals her breast, now seems to bind:
   And that fair woven net of gold refined
   Rests on her cheek and throat in happiness!
Yet still more blissful seems to me the band
   Gilt at the tips, so sweetly doth it ring
   And clasp the bosom that it serves to lace:
Yea, and the belt to such as understand,
   Bound round her waist, saith: here I'd ever cling.—
   What would my arms do in that girdle's place?
XXI.

THE SILKWORM.

D' altrui pietoso.

Kind to the world, but to itself unkind,
   A worm is born, that dying noiselessly
   Despoils itself to clothe fair limbs, and be
   In its true worth by death alone divined.
Oh, would that I might die, for her to find
   Raiment in my outworn mortality!
   That, changing like the snake, I might be free
   To cast the slough wherein I dwell confined!
Nay, were it mine, that shaggy fleece that stays,
   Woven and wrought into a vestment fair,
   Around her beauteous bosom in such bliss!
All through the day she'd clasp me! Would I were
   The shoes that bear her burden! When the ways
   Were wet with rain, her feet I then should kiss!
XXII.

WAITING IN FAITH.

Se nel volto per gli occhi

If through the eyes the heart speaks clear and true,
   I have no stronger sureties than these eyes
   For my pure love. Prithee let them suffice,
   Lord of my soul, pity to gain from you.
More tenderly perchance than is my due,
   Your spirit sees into my heart, where rise
   The flames of holy worship, nor denies

The grace reserved for those who humbly sue.
Oh, blesséd day when you at last are mine!
Let time stand still, and let noon's chariot stay;
Fixed be that moment on the dial of heaven!
That I may clasp and keep, by grace divine,
Clasp in these yearning arms and keep for aye
My heart's loved lord to me desertless given!
XXIII.

FLESH AND SPIRIT.

Ben posson gli occhi.

Well may these eyes of mine both near and far
Behold the beams that from thy beauty flow;
But, lady, feet must halt where sight may go:
We see, but cannot climb to clasp a star.
The pure ethereal soul surmounts that bar
Of flesh, and soars to where thy splendours glow,
Free through the eyes; while prisoned here below,
Though fired with fervent love, our bodies are.
Clogged with mortality and wingless, we
Cannot pursue an angel in her flight:
Only to gaze exhausts our utmost might.
Yet, if but heaven like earth incline to thee,
Let my whole body be one eye to see,
That not one part of me may miss thy sight!
XXIV.

THE DOOM OF BEAUTY.

Spirto ben nato.

Choice soul, in whom, as in a glass, we see,
Mirrored in thy pure form and delicate,
What beauties heaven and nature can create,
The paragon of all their works to be!
Fair soul, in whom love, pity, piety,
Have found a home, as from thy outward state
We clearly read, and are so rare and great
That they adorn none other like to thee!
Love takes me captive; beauty binds my soul;
Pity and mercy with their gentle eyes
Wake in my heart a hope that cannot cheat.
What law, what destiny, what fell control,
What cruelty, or late or soon, denies
That death should spare perfection so complete?
XXV.

THE TRANSFIGURATION OF BEAUTY:

A DIALOGUE WITH LOVE.

Dimmi di grazia, amor.

Nay, prithee tell me, Love, when I behold
  My lady, do mine eyes her beauty see
  In truth, or dwells that loveliness in me
  Which multiplies her grace a thousandfold?
Thou needs must know; for thou with her of old
  Comest to stir my soul's tranquillity;
  Yet would I not seek one sigh less, or be
  By loss of that loved flame more simply cold.—
The beauty thou discernest, all is hers;
  But grows in radiance as it soars on high
  Through mortal eyes unto the soul above:
'Tis there transfigured; for the soul confers
  On what she holds, her own divinity:
  And this transfigured beauty wins thy love.
XXVI.

JOY MAY KILL.

Non men gran grasia, donna.

Too much good luck no less than misery
  May kill a man condemned to mortal pain,
  If, lost to hope and chilled in every vein,
  A sudden pardon comes to set him free.
Thus thy unwonted kindness shown to me
  Amid the gloom where only sad thoughts reign,
  With too much rapture bringing light again,
  Threatens my life more than that agony.
Good news and bad may bear the self-same knife;
  And death may follow both upon their flight;
  For hearts that shrink or swell, alike will break.
Let then thy beauty, to preserve my life,
  Temper the source of this supreme delight,
  Lest joy so poignant slay a soul so weak.
XXVII.

NO ESCAPE FROM LOVE.

Non posso altra figura.

I cannot by the utmost flight of thought
  Conceive another form of air or clay,
  Wherewith against thy beauty to array

My wounded heart in armour fancy-wrought:
For, lacking thee, so low my state is brought,
That Love hath stolen all my strength away;
Whence, when I fain would halve my griefs, they weigh
With double sorrow, and I sink to nought.
Thus all in vain my soul to scape thee flies,
For ever faster flies her beauteous foe:
From the swift-footed feebly run the slow!
Yet with his hands Love wipes my weeping eyes,
Saying, this toil will end in happy cheer;
What costs the heart so much, must needs be dear!

XXVIII.

THE HEAVENLY BIRTH OF LOVE AND BEAUTY.

La vita del mie amor.

This heart of flesh feeds not with life my love:
The love wherewith I love thee hath no heart;
Nor harbours it in any mortal part,
Where erring thought or ill desire may move.
When first Love sent our souls from God above,
He fashioned me to see thee as thou art—
Pure light; and thus I find God's counterpart
In thy fair face, and feel the sting thereof.
As heat from fire, from loveliness divine
The mind that worships what recalls the sun
From whence she sprang, can be divided never:
And since thine eyes all Paradise enshrine,
Burning unto those orbs of light I run,
There where I loved thee first to dwell for ever.

XXIX.

LOVE'S DILEMMA.

I' mi credetti.

I deemed upon that day when first I knew
So many peerless beauties blent in one,
That, like an eagle gazing on the sun,
Mine eyes might fix on the least part of you.
That dream hath vanished, and my hope is flown;
For he who fain a seraph would pursue
Wingless, hath cast words to the winds, and dew
On stones, and gauged God's reason with his own.
If then my heart cannot endure the blaze
Of beauties infinite that blind these eyes,
Nor yet can bear to be from you divided,
What fate is mine? Who guides or guards my ways,

Seeing my soul, so lost and ill-betided,
Burns in your presence, in your absence dies?

XXX.

TO TOMMASO DE' CAVALIERI.

LOVE THE LIGHT-GIVER.

Veggio co' bei vostri occhi.

With your fair eyes a charming light I see,
For which my own blind eyes would peer in vain;
Stayed by your feet the burden I sustain
Which my lame feet find all too strong for me;
Wingless upon your pinions forth I fly;
Heavenward your spirit stirreth me to strain;
E'en as you will, I blush and blanch again,
Freeze in the sun, burn 'neath a frosty sky.
Your will includes and is the lord of mine;
Life to my thoughts within your heart is given;
My words begin to breathe upon your breath:
Like to the moon am I, that cannot shine
Alone; for lo! our eyes see nought in heaven
Save what the living sun illumineth.

XXXI.

To TOMMASO DE' CAVALIERI.

LOVE'S LORDSHIP.

A che più debb' io.

Why should I seek to ease intense desire
With still more tears and windy words of grief,
When heaven, or late or soon, sends no relief
To souls whom love hath robed around with fire?
Why need my aching heart to death aspire,
When all must die? Nay, death beyond belief
Unto these eyes would be both sweet and brief,
Since in my sum of woes all joys expire!
Therefore because I cannot shun the blow
I rather seek, say who must rule my breast,
Gliding between her gladness and her woe?
If only chains and bands can make me blest,
No marvel if alone and bare I go
An armèd Knight's captive and slave confessed.

XXXII.

LOVE'S EXPOSTULATION.

S' un casto amor.

If love be chaste, if virtue conquer ill,
   If fortune bind both lovers in one bond,
   If either at the other's grief despond,
   If both be governed by one life, one will;
If in two bodies one soul triumph still,
   Raising the twain from earth to heaven beyond,
   If Love with one blow and one golden wand
   Have power both smitten breasts to pierce and thrill;
If each the other love, himself forgoing,
   With such delight, such savour, and so well,
   That both to one sole end their wills combine;
If thousands of these thoughts, all thought outgoing,
   Fail the least part of their firm love to tell:
   Say, can mere angry spite this knot untwine?
XXXIII.

FIRST READING.

A PRAYER TO NATURE.

AMOR REDIVIVUS.

Perchè tuo gran bellezze.

That thy great beauty on our earth may be
   Shrined in a lady softer and more kind,
   I call on nature to collect and bind
   All those delights the slow years steal from thee,
And save them to restore the radiancy
   Of thy bright face in some fair form designed
   By heaven; and may Love ever bear in mind
   To mould her heart of grace and courtesy.
I call on nature too to keep my sighs,
   My scattered tears to take and recombine,
   And give to him who loves that fair again:
More happy he perchance shall move those eyes
   To mercy by the griefs wherewith I pine,
   Nor lose the kindness that from me is ta'en!
XXXIII.

SECOND READING.

A PRAYER TO NATURE.

AMOR REDIVIVUS.

Sol perchè tue bellezze.

If only that thy beauties here may be
    Deathless through Time that rends the wreaths he twined,
    I trust that Nature will collect and bind
    All those delights the slow years steal from thee,
And keep them for a birth more happily
    Born under better auspices, refined
    Into a heavenly form of nobler mind,
    And dowered with all thine angel purity.
Ah me! and may heaven also keep my sighs,
    My scattered tears preserve and reunite,
    And give to him who loves that fair again!
More happy he perchance shall move those eyes
    To mercy by the griefs my manhood blight,
    Nor lose the kindness that from me is ta'en!

XXXIV.

LOVE'S FURNACE.

Sì amico al freddo sasso.

So friendly is the fire to flinty stone,
    That, struck therefrom and kindled to a blaze,
    It burns the stone, and from the ash doth raise
    What lives thenceforward binding stones in one:
Kiln-hardened this resists both frost and sun,
    Acquiring higher worth for endless days—
    As the purged soul from hell returns with praise,
    Amid the heavenly host to take her throne.
E'en so the fire struck from my soul, that lay
    Close-hidden in my heart, may temper me,
    Till burned and slaked to better life I rise.
If, made mere smoke and dust, I live to-day,
    Fire-hardened I shall live eternally;
    Such gold, not iron, my spirit strikes and tries.

XXXV.

LOVE'S PARADOXES.

Sento d' un foco.

Far off with fire I feel a cold face lit,
    That makes me burn, the while itself doth freeze:
    Two fragile arms enchain me, which with ease,
    Unmoved themselves, can move weights infinite.
A soul none knows but I, most exquisite,
    That, deathless, deals me death, my spirit sees:
    I meet with one who, free, my heart doth seize:

And who alone can cheer, hath tortured it.
How can it be that from one face like thine
My own should feel effects so contrary,
Since ill comes not from things devoid of ill?
That loveliness perchance doth make me pine,
Even as the sun, whose fiery beams we see,
Inflames the world, while he is temperate still.

XXXVI.

LOVE MISINTERPRETED.

Se l'immortal desio.

If the undying thirst that purifies
Our mortal thoughts, could draw mine to the day,
Perchance the lord who now holds cruel sway
In Love's high house, would prove more kindly-wise.
But since the laws of heaven immortalise
Our souls, and doom our flesh to swift decay,
Tongue cannot tell how fair, how pure as day,
Is the soul's thirst that far beyond it lies.
How then, ah woe is me! shall that chaste fire,
Which burns the heart within me, be made known,
If sense finds only sense in what it sees?
All my fair hours are turned to miseries
With my loved lord, who minds but lies alone;
For, truth to tell, who trusts not is a liar.

XXXVII.

PERHAPS TO VITTORIA COLONNA.

LOVE'S SERVITUDE.

S' alcun legato è pur.

He who is bound by some great benefit,
As to be raised from death to life again,
How shall he recompense that gift, or gain
Freedom from servitude so infinite?
Yet if 'twere possible to pay the debt,
He'd lose that kindness which we entertain
For those who serve us well; since it is plain
That kindness needs some boon to quicken it.
Wherefore, O lady, to maintain thy grace,
So far above my fortune, what I bring
Is rather thanklessness than courtesy:
For if both met as equals face to face,
She whom I love could not be called my king;—
There is no lordship in equality.

XXXVIII.

LOVE'S VAIN EXPENSE.

Rendete a gli occhi miei.

Give back unto mine eyes, ye fount and rill,
   Those streams, not yours, that are so full and strong,
   That swell your springs, and roll your waves along
   With force unwonted in your native hill!
And thou, dense air, weighed with my sighs so chill,
   That hidest heaven's own light thick mists among,
   Give back those sighs to my sad heart, nor wrong
   My visual ray with thy dark face of ill!
Let earth give back the footprints that I wore,
   That the bare grass I spoiled may sprout again;
   And Echo, now grown deaf, my cries return!
Loved eyes, unto mine eyes those looks restore,
   And let me woo another not in vain,
   Since how to please thee I shall never learn!
XXXIX.

LOVE'S ARGUMENT WITH REASON.

La ragion meco si lamenta.

Reason laments and grieves full sore with me,
   The while I hope by loving to be blest;
   With precepts sound and true philosophy
   My shame she quickens thus within my breast:
'What else but death will that sun deal to thee—
   Nor like the phoenix in her flaming nest?'
   Yet nought avails this wise morality;
   No hand can save a suicide confessed.
I know my doom; the truth I apprehend:
   But on the other side my traitorous heart
   Slays me whene'er to wisdom's words I bend.
Between two deaths my lady stands apart:
   This death I dread; that none can comprehend.
   In this suspense body and soul must part.
XL.

FIRST READING.

LOVE'S LOADSTONE.

No so s' è la desiata luce.

I know not if it be the longed-for light

Of her first Maker which the spirit feels;
Or if a time-old memory reveals
Some other beauty for the heart's delight;
Or fame or dreams beget that vision bright,
Sweet to the eyes, which through the bosom steals,
Leaving I know not what that wounds and heals,
And now perchance hath made me weep outright.
Be this what this may be, 'tis this I seek:
Nor guide have I; nor know I where to find
That burning fire; yet some one seems to lead.
This, since I saw thee, lady, makes me weak;
A bitter-sweet sways here and there my mind,
And sure I am thine eyes this mischief breed.

XL.

SECOND READING.

LOVE'S LOADSTONE.

Non so se s' é l' immaginata luce.

I know not if it be the fancied light
Which every man or more or less doth feel;
Or if the mind and memory reveal
Some other beauty for the heart's delight;
Or if within the soul the vision bright
Of her celestial home once more doth steal,
Drawing our better thoughts with pure appeal
To the true Good above all mortal sight:
This light I long for and unguided seek;
This fire that burns my heart, I cannot find;
Nor know the way, though some one seems to lead.
This, since I saw thee, lady, makes me weak:
A bitter-sweet sways here and there my mind;
And sure I am thine eyes this mischief breed.

XLI.

LIGHT AND DARKNESS.

Colui che fece.

He who ordained, when first the world began,
Time, that was not before creation's hour,
Divided it, and gave the sun's high power
To rule the one, the moon the other span:
Thence fate and changeful chance and fortune's ban
Did in one moment down on mortals shower:
To me they portioned darkness for a dower;
Dark hath my lot been since I was a man.

Myself am ever mine own counterfeit;
   And as deep night grows still more dim and dun,
   So still of more misdoing must I rue:
Meanwhile this solace to my soul is sweet,
   That my black night doth make more clear the sun
   Which at your birth was given to wait on you.
XLII.

SACRED NIGHT.

Ogni van chiuso.

All hollow vaults and dungeons sealed from sight,
   All caverns circumscribed with roof and wall,
   Defend dark Night, though noon around her fall,
   From the fierce play of solar day-beams bright.
But if she be assailed by fire or light,
   Her powers divine are nought; they tremble all
   Before things far more vile and trivial—
   Even a glow-worm can confound their might.
The earth that lies bare to the sun, and breeds
   A thousand germs that burgeon and decay—
   This earth is wounded by the ploughman's share:
But only darkness serves for human seeds;
   Night therefore is more sacred far than day,
   Since man excels all fruits however fair.
XLIII.

THE IMPEACHMENT OF NIGHT.

Perchè Febo non torce.

What time bright Phoebus doth not stretch and bend
   His shining arms around this terrene sphere,
   The people call that season dark and drear
   Night, for the cause they do not comprehend.
So weak is Night that if our hand extend
   A glimmering torch, her shadows disappear,
   Leaving her dead; like frailest gossamere,
   Tinder and steel her mantle rive and rend.
Nay, if this Night be anything at all,
   Sure she is daughter of the sun and earth;
   This holds, the other spreads that shadowy pall.
Howbeit they err who praise this gloomy birth,
   So frail and desolate and void of mirth
   That one poor firefly can her might appal.
XLIV.

THE DEFENCE OF NIGHT.

O nott' o dolce tempo.

O night, O sweet though sombre span of time!—
All things find rest upon their journey's end—
Whoso hath praised thee, well doth apprehend;
And whoso honours thee, hath wisdom's prime.
Our cares thou canst to quietude sublime;
For dews and darkness are of peace the friend:
Often by thee in dreams upborne, I wend
From earth to heaven, where yet I hope to climb.
Thou shade of Death, through whom the soul at length
Shuns pain and sadness hostile to the heart,
Whom mourners find their last and sure relief!
Thou dost restore our suffering flesh to strength,
Driest our tears, assuagest every smart,
Purging the spirits of the pure from grief.
XLV.

LOVE FEEDS THE FLAME OF AGE.

Quand' il servo il signior.

When masters bind a slave with cruel chain,
And keep him hope-forlorn in bondage pent,
Use tames his temper to imprisonment,
And hardly would he fain be free again.
Use curbs the snake and tiger, and doth train
Fierce woodland lions to bear chastisement;
And the young artist, all with toil forspent,
By constant use a giant's strength doth gain
But with the force of flame it is not so:
For while fire sucks the sap of the green wood,
It warms a frore old man and makes him grow;
With such fine heat of youth and lustihood
Filling his heart and teaching it to glow,
That love enfolds him with beatitude.
If then in playful mood
He sport and jest, old age need no man blame;
For loving things divine implies no shame.
The soul that knows her aim,
Sins not by loving God's own counterfeit—
Due measure kept, and bounds, and order meet.
XLVI.

LOVE'S FLAME DOTH FEED ON AGE.

Se da' prim' anni.

If some mild heat of love in youth confessed
   Burns a fresh heart with swift consuming fire,
   What will the force be of a flame more dire
   Shut up within an old man's cindery breast?
If the mere lapse of lengthening years hath pressed
   So sorely that life, strength, and vigour tire,
   How shall he fare who must ere long expire,
   When to old age is added love's unrest?
Weak as myself, he will be whirled away
   Like dust by winds kind in their cruelty,
   Robbing the loathly worm of its last prey.
A little flame consumed and fed on me
   In my green age: now that the wood is dry,
   What hope against this fire more fierce have I?
XLVII.

BEAUTY'S INTOLERABLE SPLENDOUR.

Se 'l foco alla bellezza.

If but the fire that lightens in thine eyes
   Were equal with their beauty, all the snow
   And frost of all the world would melt and glow
   Like brands that blaze beneath fierce tropic skies.
But heaven in mercy to our miseries
   Dulls and divides the fiery beams that flow
   From thy great loveliness, that we may go
   Through this stern mortal life in tranquil wise.
Thus beauty burns not with consuming rage;
   For so much only of the heavenly light
   Inflames our love as finds a fervent heart.
This is my case, lady, in sad old age:
   If seeing thee, I do not die outright,
   'Tis that I feel thy beauty but in part.
XLVIII.

LOVE'S EVENING.

Se 'l troppo indugio.

What though long waiting wins more happiness
   Than petulant desire is wont to gain,
   My luck in latest age hath brought me pain,
   Thinking how brief must be an old man's bliss.
Heaven, if it heed our lives, can hardly bless
   This fire of love when frosts are wont to reign:
   For so I love thee, lady, and my strain
   Of tears through age exceeds in tenderness.
Yet peradventure though my day is done,—

Though nearly past the setting mid thick cloud
And frozen exhalations sinks my sun,—
If love to only mid-day be allowed,
And I an old man in my evening burn,
You, lady, still my night to noon may turn.
XLIX.

LOVE'S EXCUSE.

Dal dolcie pianto.

From happy tears to woeful smiles, from peace
Eternal to a brief and hollow truce,
How have I fallen!—when 'tis truth we lose,
Sense triumphs o'er all adverse impulses.
I know not if my heart bred this disease,
That still more pleasing grows with growing use;
Or else thy face, thine eyes, which stole the hues
And fires of Paradise—less fair than these.
Thy beauty is no mortal thing; 'twas sent
From heaven on high to make our earth divine:
Wherefore, though wasting, burning, I'm content;
For in thy sight what could I do but pine?
If God himself thus rules my destiny,
Who, when I die, can lay the blame on thee?
L.

IN LOVE'S OWN TIME.

S' i' avessi creduto.

Had I but earlier known that from the eyes
Of that bright soul that fires me like the sun,
I might have drawn new strength my race to run,
Burning as burns the phoenix ere it dies;
Even as the stag or lynx or leopard flies
To seek his pleasure and his pain to shun,
Each word, each smile of her would I have won,
Flying where now sad age all flight denies.
Yet why complain? For even now I find
In that glad angel's face, so full of rest,
Health and content, heart's ease and peace of mind
Perchance I might have been less simply blest,
Finding her sooner: if 'tis age alone
That lets me soar with her to seek God's throne.
LI.

FIRST READING.

LOVE IN YOUTH AND AGE.

Tornami al tempo.

Bring back the time when blind desire ran free,
With bit and rein too loose to curb his flight;
Give back the buried face, once angel-bright,
That hides in earth all comely things from me;
Bring back those journeys ta'en so toilsomely,
So toilsome-slow to one whose hairs are white;
Those tears and flames that in one breast unite;
If thou wilt once more take thy fill of me!
Yet Love! Suppose it true that thou dost thrive
Only on bitter honey-dews of tears.
Small profit hast thou of a weak old man.
My soul that toward the other shore doth strive,
Wards off thy darts with shafts of holier fears;
And fire feeds ill on brands no breath can fan.

LI.

SECOND READING.

LOVE IN YOUTH AND AGE.

Tornami al tempo.

Bring back the time when glad desire ran free
With bit and rein too loose to curb his flight,
The tears and flames that in one breast unite,
If thou art fain once more to conquer me!
Bring back those journeys ta'en so toilsomely,
So toilsome-slow to him whose hairs are white!
Give back the buried face once angel-bright,
That taxed all Nature's art and industry.
O Love! an old man finds it hard to chase
Thy flying pinions! Thou hast left thy nest;
Nor is my heart as light as heretofore.
Put thy gold arrows to the string once more:
Then if Death hear my prayer and grant me grace,
My grief I shall forget, again made blest.

LII.

CELESTIAL LOVE.

Non vider gli occhi miei.

I saw no mortal beauty with these eyes
When perfect peace in thy fair eyes I found;
But far within, where all is holy ground,

My soul felt Love, her comrade of the skies:
For she was born with God in Paradise;
Else should we still to transient loves be bound;
But, finding these so false, we pass beyond
Unto the Love of Loves that never dies.
Nay, things that die, cannot assuage the thirst
Of souls undying; nor Eternity
Serves Time, where all must fade that flourisheth.
Sense is not love, but lawlessness accurst:
This kills the soul; while our love lifts on high
Our friends on earth—higher in heaven through death.

LIII.

CELESTIAL AND EARTHLY LOVE.

Non è sempre di colpa.

Love is not always harsh and deadly sin:
If it be love of loveliness divine,
It leaves the heart all soft and infantine
For rays of God's own grace to enter in.
Love fits the soul with wings, and bids her win
Her flight aloft nor e'er to earth decline;
'Tis the first step that leads her to the shrine
Of Him who slakes the thirst that burns within.
The love of that whereof I speak, ascends:
Woman is different far; the love of her
But ill befits a heart all manly wise.
The one love soars, the other downward tends;
The soul lights this, while that the senses stir,
And still his arrow at base quarry flies.

LIV.

LOVE LIFTS TO GOD.

Veggio nel tuo bel viso.

From thy fair face I learn, O my loved lord,
That which no mortal tongue can rightly say;
The soul, imprisoned in her house of clay,
Holpen by thee to God hath often soared:
And though the vulgar, vain, malignant horde
Attribute what their grosser wills obey,
Yet shall this fervent homage that I pay,
This love, this faith, pure joys for us afford.
Lo, all the lovely things we find on earth,
Resemble for the soul that rightly sees,
That source of bliss divine which gave us birth:
Nor have we first-fruits or remembrances

Of heaven elsewhere. Thus, loving loyally,
I rise to God and make death sweet by thee.

LV.

LOVE'S ENTREATY.

Tu sa' ch' i' so, Signor mie.

Thou knowest, love, I know that thou dost know
That I am here more near to thee to be,
And knowest that I know thou knowest me:
What means it then that we are sundered so?
If they are true, these hopes that from thee flow,
If it is real, this sweet expectancy,
Break down the wall that stands 'twixt me and thee;
For pain in prison pent hath double woe.
Because in thee I love, O my loved lord,
What thou best lovest, be not therefore stern:
Souls burn for souls, spirits to spirits cry!
I seek the splendour in thy fair face stored;
Yet living man that beauty scarce can learn,
And he who fain would find it, first must die.

LVI.

FIRST READING.

HEAVEN-BORN BEAUTY.

Per ritornar là.

As one who will reseek her home of light,
Thy form immortal to this prison-house
Descended, like an angel piteous,
To heal all hearts and make the whole world bright.
'Tis this that thralls my soul in love's delight,
Not thy clear face of beauty glorious;
For he who harbours virtue, still will choose
To love what neither years nor death can blight.
So fares it ever with things high and rare
Wrought in the sweat of nature; heaven above
Showers on their birth the blessings of her prime:
Nor hath God deigned to show Himself elsewhere
More clearly than in human forms sublime;
Which, since they image Him, alone I love.

LVI.

SECOND READING.

HEAVEN-BORN BEAUTY.

Venne, non so ben donde.

It came, I know not whence, from far above,
That clear immortal flame that still doth rise
Within thy sacred breast, and fills the skies,
And heals all hearts, and adds to heaven new love.
This burns me, this, and the pure light thereof;
Not thy fair face, thy sweet untroubled eyes:
For love that is not love for aught that dies,
Dwells in the soul where no base passions move.
If then such loveliness upon its own
Should graft new beauties in a mortal birth,
The sheath bespeaks the shining blade within.
To gain our love God hath not clearer shown
Himself elsewhere: thus heaven doth vie with earth
To make thee worthy worship without sin.
LVII.

FIRST READING.

CARNAL AND SPIRITUAL LOVE.

Passa per gli occhi.

Swift through the eyes unto the heart within
All lovely forms that thrall our spirit stray;
So smooth and broad and open is the way
That thousands and not hundreds enter in.
Burdened with scruples and weighed down with sin,
These mortal beauties fill me with dismay;
Nor find I one that doth not strive to stay
My soul on transient joy, or lets me win
The heaven I yearn for. Lo, when erring love—
Who fills the world, howe'er his power we shun,
Else were the world a grave and we undone—
Assails the soul, if grace refuse to fan
Our purged desires and make them soar above,
What grief it were to have been born a man!
LVII.

SECOND READING.

CARNAL AND SPIRITUAL LOVE.

Passa per gli occhi.

Swift through the eyes unto the heart within
All lovely forms that thrall our spirit stray;

So smooth and broad and open is the way
That thousands and not hundreds enter in
Of every age and sex: whence I begin,
Burdened with griefs, but more with dull dismay,
To fear; nor find mid all their bright array
One that with full content my heart may win.
If mortal beauty be the food of love,
It came not with the soul from heaven, and thus
That love itself must be a mortal fire:
But if love reach to nobler hopes above,
Thy love shall scorn me not nor dread desire
That seeks a carnal prey assailing us.

LVIII.

LOVE AND DEATH.

Ognor che l' idol mio.

Whene'er the idol of these eyes appears
Unto my musing heart so weak and strong,
Death comes between her and my soul ere long
Chasing her thence with troops of gathering fears.
Nathless this violence my spirit cheers
With better hope than if she had no wrong;
While Love invincible arrays the throng
Of dauntless thoughts, and thus harangues his peers:
But once, he argues, can a mortal die;
But once be born: and he who dies afire,
What shall he gain if erst he dwelt with me?
That burning love whereby the soul flies free,
Doth lure each fervent spirit to aspire
Like gold refined in flame to God on high.

LIX.

LOVE IS A REFINER'S FIRE.

Non più ch' 'l foco il fabbro.

It is with fire that blacksmiths iron subdue
Unto fair form, the image of their thought:
Nor without fire hath any artist wrought
Gold to its utmost purity of hue.
Nay, nor the unmatched phoenix lives anew,
Unless she burn: if then I am distraught
By fire, I may to better life be brought
Like those whom death restores nor years undo.
The fire whereof I speak, is my great cheer;
Such power it hath to renovate and raise
Me who was almost numbered with the dead;

And since by nature fire doth find its sphere
Soaring aloft, and I am all ablaze,
Heavenward with it my flight must needs be sped.
LX.

FIRST READING.

LOVE'S JUSTIFICATION.

Ben può talor col mio.

Sometimes my love I dare to entertain
With soaring hope not over-credulous;
Since if all human loves were impious,
Unto what end did God the world ordain?
For loving thee what license is more plain
Than that I praise thereby the glorious
Source of all joys divine, that comfort us
In thee, and with chaste fires our soul sustain?
False hope belongs unto that love alone
Which with declining beauty wanes and dies,
And, like the face it worships, fades away.
That hope is true which the pure heart hath known,
Which alters not with time or death's decay,
Yielding on earth earnest of Paradise.
LX.

SECOND READING.

LOVE'S JUSTIFICATION.

Ben può talor col casto.

It must be right sometimes to entertain
Chaste love with hope not over-credulous;
Since if all human loves were impious,
Unto what end did God the world ordain?
If I love thee and bend beneath thy reign,
'Tis for the sake of beauty glorious
Which in thine eyes divine is stored for us,
And drives all evil thought from its domain.
That is not love whose tyranny we own
In loveliness that every moment dies;
Which, like the face it worships, fades away:
True love is that which the pure heart hath known,
Which alters not with time or death's decay,
Yielding on earth earnest of Paradise.
LXI.

AFTER THE DEATH OF VITTORIA COLONNA.

IRREPARABLE LOSS.

Se 'l mie rozzo martello.

When my rude hammer to the stubborn stone
Gives human shape, now that, now this, at will,
Following his hand who wields and guides it still,
It moves upon another's feet alone:
But that which dwells in heaven, the world doth fill
With beauty by pure motions of its own;
And since tools fashion tools which else were none,
Its life makes all that lives with living skill.
Now, for that every stroke excels the more
The higher at the forge it doth ascend,
Her soul that fashioned mine hath sought the skies:
Wherefore unfinished I must meet my end,
If God, the great artificer, denies
That aid which was unique on earth before.

LXII.

AFTER THE DEATH OF VITTORIA COLONNA.

LOVE'S TRIUMPH OVER DEATH.

Quand' el ministro de' sospir.

When she who was the source of all my sighs,
Fled from the world, herself, my straining sight,
Nature who gave us that unique delight,
Was sunk in shame, and we had weeping eyes.
Yet shall not vauntful Death enjoy this prize,
This sun of suns which then he veiled in night;
For Love hath triumphed, lifting up her light
On earth and mid the saints in Paradise.
What though remorseless and impiteous doom
Deemed that the music of her deeds would die,
And that her splendour would be sunk in gloom,
The poet's page exalts her to the sky
With life more living in the lifeless tomb,
And death translates her soul to reign on high.

LXIII.

AFTER THE DEATH OF VITTORIA COLONNA.

AFTER SUNSET.

Be' mi dove'.

Well might I in those days so fortunate,
What time the sun lightened my path above,
Have soared from earth to heaven, raised by her love
Who winged my labouring soul and sweetened fate.
That sun hath set; and I with hope elate
Who deemed that those bright days would never move,
Find that my thankless soul, deprived thereof,
Declines to death, while heaven still bars the gate.
Love lent me wings; my path was like a stair;
A lamp unto my feet, that sun was given;
And death was safety and great joy to find.
But dying now, I shall not climb to heaven;
Nor can mere memory cheer my heart's despair:—
What help remains when hope is left behind?

LXIV.

AFTER THE DEATH OF VITTORIA COLONNA.

A WASTED BRAND.

Qual maraviglia è.

If being near the fire I burned with it,
Now that its flame is quenched and doth not show,
What wonder if I waste within and glow,
Dwindling away to cinders bit by bit?
While still it burned, I saw so brightly lit
That splendour whence I drew my grievous woe,
That from its sight alone could pleasure flow,
And death and torment both seemed exquisite.
But now that heaven hath robbed me of the blaze
Of that great fire which burned and nourished me,
A coal that smoulders 'neath the ash am I.
Unless Love furnish wood fresh flames to raise,
I shall expire with not one spark to see,
So quickly into embers do I die!

LXV.

TO GIORGIO VASARI.

ON THE BRINK OF DEATH.

Giunto è già.

Now hath my life across a stormy sea
Like a frail bark reached that wide port where all
Are bidden, ere the final reckoning fall
Of good and evil for eternity.

Now know I well how that fond phantasy
Which made my soul the worshipper and thrall
Of earthly art, is vain; how criminal
Is that which all men seek unwillingly.
Those amorous thoughts which were so lightly dressed,
What are they when the double death is nigh?
The one I know for sure, the other dread.
Painting nor sculpture now can lull to rest
My soul that turns to His great love on high,
Whose arms to clasp us on the cross were spread.
LXVI.

TO GIORGIO VASARI.

VANITY OF VANITIES.

Le favole del mondo.

The fables of the world have filched away
The time I had for thinking upon God;
His grace lies buried 'neath oblivion's sod,
Whence springs an evil crop of sins alway.
What makes another wise, leads me astray,
Slow to discern the bad path I have trod:
Hope fades; but still desire ascends that God
May free me from self-love, my sure decay.
Shorten half-way my road to heaven from earth!
Dear Lord, I cannot even half-way rise,
Unless Thou help me on this pilgrimage.
Teach me to hate the world so little worth,
And all the lovely things I clasp and prize;
That endless life, ere death, may be my wage.
LXVII.

A PRAYER FOR FAITH.

Non è più bassa.

There's not on earth a thing more vile and base
Than, lacking Thee, I feel myself to be:
For pardon prays my own debility,
Yearning in vain to lift me to Thy face.
Stretch to me, Lord, that chain whose links enlace
All heavenly gifts and all felicity—
Faith, whereunto I strive perpetually,
Yet cannot find (my fault) her perfect grace.
That gift of gifts, the rarer 'tis, the more
I count it great; more great, because to earth
Without it neither peace nor joy is given.

If Thou Thy blood so lovingly didst pour,
   Let not that bounty fail or suffer dearth,
   Withholding Faith that opes the doors of heaven.

LXVIII.

TO MONSIGNOR LODOVICO BECCADELLI.

URBINO.

Per croce e grazia.

God's grace, the cross, our troubles multiplied,
Will make us meet in heaven, full well I know:
Yet ere we yield our breath, on earth below
Why need a little solace be denied?
Though seas and mountains and rough ways divide
Our feet asunder, neither frost nor snow
Can make the soul her ancient love forgo;
Nor chains nor bonds the wings of thought have tied.
Borne by these wings with thee I dwell for aye,
And weep, and of my dead Urbino talk,
Who, were he living, now perchance would be,
For so 'twas planned, thy guest as well as I:
Warned by his death another way I walk
To meet him where he waits to live with me.

LXIX.

WAITING FOR DEATH.

Di morte certo.

My death must come; but when, I do not know:
Life's short, and little life remains for me:
Fain would my flesh abide; my soul would flee
Heavenward, for still she calls on me to go.
Blind is the world; and evil here below
O'erwhelms and triumphs over honesty:
The light is quenched; quenched too is bravery:
Lies reign, and truth hath ceased her face to show.
When will that day dawn, Lord, for which he waits
Who trusts in Thee? Lo, this prolonged delay
Destroys all hope and robs the soul of life.
Why streams the light from those celestial gates,
If death prevent the day of grace, and stay
Our souls for ever in the toils of strife?

LXX.

A PRAYER FOR STRENGTH.

Carico d'anni.

Burdened with years and full of sinfulness,
With evil custom grown inveterate,
Both deaths I dread that close before me wait,
Yet feed my heart on poisonous thoughts no less.
No strength I find in mine own feebleness
To change or life or love or use or fate,
Unless Thy heavenly guidance come, though late,
Which only helps and stays our nothingness.
'Tis not enough, dear Lord, to make me yearn
For that celestial home, where yet my soul
May be new made, and not, as erst, of nought:
Nay, ere Thou strip her mortal vestment, turn
My steps toward the steep ascent, that whole
And pure before Thy face she may be brought.
LXXI.

A PRAYER FOR PURIFICATION.

Forse perchè d' altrui.

Perchance that I might learn what pity is,
That I might laugh at erring men no more,
Secure in my own strength as heretofore,
My soul hath fallen from her state of bliss:
Nor know I under any flag but this
How fighting I may 'scape those perils sore,
Or how survive the rout and horrid roar
Of adverse hosts, if I Thy succour miss.
O flesh! O blood! O cross! O pain extreme!
By you may those foul sins be purified,
Wherein my fathers were, and I was born!
Lo, Thou alone art good: let Thy supreme
Pity my state of evil cleanse and hide—
So near to death, so far from God, forlorn.
LXXII.

A PRAYER FOR AID.

Deh fammiti vedere.

Oh, make me see Thee, Lord, where'er I go!
If mortal beauty sets my soul on fire,
That flame when near to Thine must needs expire,
And I with love of only Thee shall glow.
Dear Lord, Thy help I seek against this woe,
These torments that my spirit vex and tire;
Thou only with new strength canst re-inspire

My will, my sense, my courage faint and low.
Thou gavest me on earth this soul divine;
And Thou within this body weak and frail
Didst prison it—how sadly there to live!
How can I make its lot less vile than mine?
Without Thee, Lord, all goodness seems to fail.
To alter fate is God's prerogative.

LXXIII.

AT THE FOOT OF THE CROSS.

Scarco d' un' importuna.

Freed from a burden sore and grievous band,
Dear Lord, and from this wearying world untied,
Like a frail bark I turn me to Thy side,
As from a fierce storm to a tranquil land.
Thy thorns, Thy nails, and either bleeding hand,
With Thy mild gentle piteous face, provide
Promise of help and mercies multiplied,
And hope that yet my soul secure may stand.
Let not Thy holy eyes be just to see
My evil past, Thy chastened ears to hear
And stretch the arm of judgment to my crime:
Let Thy blood only lave and succour me,
Yielding more perfect pardon, better cheer,
As older still I grow with lengthening time.

LXXIV.

FIRST READING.

A PRAYER FOR GRACE IN DEATH.

S' avvien che spesso.

What though strong love of life doth flatter me
With hope of yet more years on earth to stay,
Death none the less draws nearer day by day,
Who to sad souls alone comes lingeringly.
Yet why desire long life and jollity,
If in our griefs alone to God we pray?
Glad fortune, length of days, and pleasure slay
The soul that trusts to their felicity.
Then if at any hour through grace divine
The fiery shafts of love and faith that cheer
And fortify the soul, my heart assail,
Since nought achieve these mortal powers of mine,
Straight may I wing my way to heaven; for here
With lengthening days good thoughts and wishes fail.

LXXIV.

SECOND READING.

A PRAYER FOR GRACE IN DEATH.

Parmi che spesso.

Ofttimes my great desire doth flatter me
With hope on earth yet many years to stay:
Still Death, the more I love it, day by day
Takes from the life I love so tenderly.
What better time for that dread change could be,
If in our griefs alone to God we pray?
Oh, lead me, Lord, oh, lead me far away
From every thought that lures my soul from Thee!
Yea, if at any hour, through grace of Thine,
The fervent zeal of love and faith that cheer
And fortify the soul, my heart assail.
Since nought achieve these mortal powers of mine,
Plant, like a saint in heaven, that virtue here;
For, lacking Thee, all good must faint and fail.
LXXV.

HEART-COLDNESS.

Vorrei voler, Signior.

Fain would I wish what my heart cannot will:
Between it and the fire a veil of ice
Deadens the fire, so that I deal in lies;
My words and actions are discordant still.
I love Thee with my tongue, then mourn my fill;
For love warms not my heart, nor can I rise,
Or ope the doors of Grace, who from the skies
Might flood my soul, and pride and passion kill.
Rend Thou the veil, dear Lord! Break Thou that wall
Which with its stubbornness retards the rays
Of that bright sun this earth hath dulled for me!
Send down Thy promised light to cheer and fall
On Thy fair spouse, that I with love may blaze,
And, free from doubt, my heart feel only Thee!
LXXVI.

THE DEATH OF CHRIST.

Non fur men lieti.

Not less elate than smitten with wild woe

To see not them but Thee by death undone,
Were those blest souls, when Thou above the sun
Didst raise, by dying, men that lay so low:
Elate, since freedom from all ills that flow
From their first fault for Adam's race was won;
Sore smitten, since in torment fierce God's son
Served servants on the cruel cross below.
Heaven showed she knew Thee, who Thou wert and whence,
Veiling her eyes above the riven earth;
The mountains trembled and the seas were troubled.
He took the Fathers from hell's darkness dense:
The torments of the damnéd fiends redoubled:
Man only joyed, who gained baptismal birth.

LXXVII.

THE BLOOD OF CHRIST.

Mentre m' attrista.

Mid weariness and woe I find some cheer
In thinking of the past, when I recall
My weakness and my sins, and reckon all
The vain expense of days that disappear:
This cheers by making, ere I die, more clear
The frailty of what men delight miscall;
But saddens me to think how rarely fall
God's grace and mercies in life's latest year.
For though Thy promises our faith compel,
Yet, Lord, what man shall venture to maintain
That pity will condone our long neglect?
Still from Thy blood poured forth we know full well
How without measure was Thy martyr's pain,
How measureless the gifts we dare expect.

THE SONNETS OF TOMMASO CAMPANELLA

I.

THE PROEM.

Io che nacqui dal Senno.

Born of God's Wisdom and Philosophy,
Keen lover of true beauty and true good,
I call the vain self-traitorous multitude
Back to my mother's milk; for it is she,
Faithful to God her spouse, who nourished me,
Making me quick and active to intrude
Within the inmost veil, where I have viewed
And handled all things in eternity.

If the whole world's our home where we may run,
Up, friends, forsake those secondary schools
Which give grains, units, inches for the whole!
If facts surpass mere words, melt pride of soul,
And pain, and ignorance that hardens fools,
Here in the fire I've stolen from the Sun!

II.

TO THE POETS.

In superbia il valor.

Valour to pride hath turned; grave holiness
To vile hypocrisy; all gentle ways
To empty forms; sound sense to idle lays;
Pure love to heat; beauty to paint and dress:—
Thanks to you, Poets! you who sing the praise
Of fabled knights, foul fires, lies, nullities;
Not virtue, nor the wrapped sublimities
Of God, as bards were wont in those old days.
How far more wondrous than your phantasies
Are Nature's works, how far more sweet to sing!
Thus taught, the soul falsehood and truth descries.
That tale alone is worth the pondering,
Which hath not smothered history in lies,
And arms the soul against each sinful thing.

III.

THE UNIVERSE.

Il mondo è un animal.

The world's a living creature, whole and great,
God's image, praising God whose type it is;
We are imperfect worms, vile families,
That in its belly have our low estate.
If we know not its love, its intellect,
Neither the worm within my belly seeks
To know me, but his petty mischief wreaks:—
Thus it behoves us to be circumspect.
Again, the earth is a great animal,
Within the greatest; we are like the lice
Upon its body, doing harm as they.
Proud men, lift up your eyes; on you I call:
Measure each being's worth; and thence be wise;
Learning what part in the great scheme you play!

IV.

THE SOUL.

Dentro un pugno di cervel.

A handful of brain holds me: I consume
So much that all the books the world contains,
Cannot allay my furious famine-pains:—
What feasts were mine! Yet hunger is my doom.
With one world Aristarchus fed my greed;
This finished, others Metrodorus gave;
Yet, stirred by restless yearning, still I crave:
The more I know, the more to learn I need.
Thus I'm an image of that Sire in whom
All beings are, like fishes in the sea;
That one true object of the loving mind.
Reasoning may reach Him, like a shaft shot home;
The Church may guide; but only blest is he
Who loses self in God, God's self to find.

V.

THE BOOK OF NATURE.

Il mondo è il libro.

The world's the book where the eternal Sense
Wrote his own thoughts; the living temple where,
Painting his very self, with figures fair
He filled the whole immense circumference.
Here then should each man read, and gazing find
Both how to live and govern, and beware
Of godlessness; and, seeing God all-where,
Be bold to grasp the universal mind.
But we tied down to books and temples dead,
Copied with countless errors from the life,—
These nobler than that school sublime we call.
O may our senseless souls at length be led
To truth by pain, grief, anguish, trouble, strife!
Turn we to read the one original!

VI.

AN EXHORTATION TO MANKIND.

Abitator del mondo.

Ye dwellers on this world, to the first Mind
Exalt your eyes; and ye shall see how low
Vile Tyranny, wearing the glorious show
Of nobleness and worth, keeps you confined.
Then look at proud Hypocrisy, entwined
With lies and snares, who once taught men to know

The fear of God. Next to the Sophists go,
Traitors to thought and reason, jugglers blind.
Keen Socrates to quell the Sophists came:
To quell the Tyrants, Cato just and rough:
To quell the Hypocrites, Christ, heaven's own flame.
But to unmask fraud, sacrilege, and lies,
Or boldly rush on death, is not enough;
Unless we all taste God, made inly wise.
VII.

THE BROOD OF IGNORANCE.

Io nacqui a debellar.

To quell three Titan evils I was made,—
Tyranny, Sophistry, Hypocrisy;
Whence I perceive with what wise harmony
Themis on me Love, Power, and Wisdom laid.
These are the basements firm whereon is stayed,
Supreme and strong, our new philosophy;
The antidotes against that trinal lie
Wherewith the burdened world groaning is weighed.
Famine, war, pestilence, fraud, envy, pride,
Injustice, idleness, lust, fury, fear,
Beneath these three great plagues securely hide.
Grounded on blind self-love, the offspring dear
Of Ignorance, they flourish and abide:—
Wherefore to root up Ignorance I'm here!
VIII.

SELF-LOVE.

Credulo il proprio amor.

Self-love fools man with false opinion
That earth, air, water, fire, the stars we see,
Though stronger and more beautiful than we,
Feel nought, love not, but move for us alone.
Then all the tribes of earth except his own
Seem to him senseless, rude—God lets them be:
To kith and kin next shrinks his sympathy,
Till in the end loves only self each one.
Learning he shuns that he may live at ease;
And since the world is little to his mind,
God and God's ruling Forethought he denies.
Craft he calls wisdom; and, perversely blind,
Seeking to reign, erects new deities:
At last 'I make the Universe!' he cries.
IX.

LOVE OF SELF AND GOD.

Questo amor singolar.

This love of self sinks man in sinful sloth:
   Yet, if he seek to live, he needs must feign
   Sense, goodness, courage. Thus he dwells in pain,
   A sphinx, twy-souled, a false self-stunted growth.
Honours, applause, and wealth these torments soothe;
   Till jealousy, contrasting his foul stain
   With virtues eminent, by spur and rein
   Drives him to slay, steal, poison, break his oath.
But he who loves our common Father, hath
   All men for brothers, and with God doth joy
   In whatsoever worketh for their bliss.
Good Francis called the birds upon his path
   Brethren; to him the fishes were not coy.—
   Oh, blest is he who comprehendeth this!

X.

EARTHLY AND DIVINE LOVE.

Se Dio ci dà la vita.

God gives us life, and God our life preserves;
   Nay, all our happiness on Him doth rest:
   Why then should love of God inflame man's breast
   Less than his lady and the lord he serves?
Through mean and wanton ignorance he swerves,
   And worships a false Good, divinely dressed;
   Love cannot soar to what it never guessed,
   But stoops its flight, and the thralled soul unnerves.
Here too is man deceived. He yields his own
   To spend on others. Yet in vile delight
   God's splendour still shines through love's earthliness.
But we embrace the loss, the lure alone
   Love fools us with. That glimpse of heavenly light,
   That foretaste of eternal Good, we miss.

XI.

THE PHILOSOPHER.

Gran fortuna è 'l saper.

Wisdom is riches great and great estate,
   Far above wealth; nor are the wise unblest
   If born of lineage vile or race oppressed:
   These by their doom sublime they illustrate.

They have their griefs for guerdon, to dilate
Their name and glory; nay, the cross, the sword
Make them to be like saints or God adored;
And gladness greets them in the frowns of fate:
For joys and sorrows are their dear delight;
Even as a lover takes the weal and woe
Felt for his lady. Such is wisdom's might.
But wealth still vexes fools; more vile they grow
By being noble; and their luckless light
With each new misadventure burns more low.

XII.

A PARABLE OF WISE MEN AND THE WORLD.

Gli astrologi antevista.

Once on a time the astronomers foresaw
The coming of a star to madden men:
Thus warned they fled the land, thinking that when
The folk were crazed, they'd hold the reins of law
When they returned the realm to overawe,
They prayed those maniacs to quit cave and den,
And use their old good customs once again;
But these made answer with fist, tooth, and claw:
So that the wise men were obliged to rule
Themselves like lunatics to shun grim death,
Seeing the biggest maniac now was king.
Stifling their sense, they lived, aping the fool,
In public praising act and word and thing
Just as the whims of madmen swayed their breath.

XIII.

THE WORLD'S A STAGE.

Nel teatro del mondo.

The world's a theatre: age after age,
Souls masked and muffled in their fleshly gear
Before the supreme audience appear,
As Nature, God's own Art, appoints the stage.
Each plays the part that is his heritage;
From choir to choir they pass, from sphere to sphere,
And deck themselves with joy or sorry cheer,
As Fate the comic playwright fills the page.
None do or suffer, be they cursed or blest,
Aught otherwise than the great Wisdom wrote
To gladden each and all who gave Him mirth,
When we at last to sea or air or earth
Yielding these masks that weal or woe denote,

In God shall see who spoke and acted best.

XIV.

THE HUMAN COMEDY.

Natura dal Signor.

Nature, by God directed, formed in space
The universal comedy we see;
Wherein each star, each man, each entity,
Each living creature, hath its part and place:
And when the play is over, it shall be
That God will judge with justice and with grace.—
Aping this art divine, the human race
Plans for itself on earth a comedy:
It makes kings, priests, slaves, heroes for the eyes
Of vulgar folk; and gives them masks to play
Their several parts—not wisely, as we see;
For impious men too oft we canonise,
And kill the saints; while spurious lords array
Their hosts against the real nobility.

XV.

THE TRUE KINGS.

Neron fu Re.

Nero was king by accident in show;
But Socrates by nature in good sooth;
By right of both Augustus; luck and truth
Less perfectly were blent in Scipio.
The spurious prince still seeks to extirpate
The seed of natures born imperial—
Like Herod, Caiaphas, Meletus, all
Who by bad acts sustain their stolen state.
Slaves whose souls tell them that they are but slaves,
Strike those whose native kinghood all can see:
Martyrdom is the stamp of royalty.
Dead though they be, these govern from their graves:
The tyrants fall, nor can their laws remain;
While Paul and Peter rise o'er Rome to reign.

XVI.

WHAT MAKES A KING.

Chi pennelli have e colori.

He who hath brush and colours, and chance-wise
Doth daub, befouling walls and canvases,

Is not a painter; but, unhelped by these,
He who in art is masterful and wise.
Cowls and the tonsure do not make a friar;
Nor make a king wide realms and pompous wars;
But he who is all Jesus, Pallas, Mars,
Though he be slave or base-born, wears the tiar.
Man is not born crowned like the natural king
Of beasts, for beasts by this investiture
Have need to know the head they must obey;
Wherefore a commonwealth fits men, I say,
Or else a prince whose worth is tried and sure,
Not proved by sloth or false imagining.

XVII.

TO JESUS CHRIST.

I tuo' seguaci.

Thy followers to-day are less like Thee,
The crucified, than those who made Thee die,
Good Jesus, wandering all ways awry
From rules prescribed in Thy wise charity.
The saints now most esteemed love lying lips,
Lust, strife, injustice; sweet to them the cry
Drawn forth by monstrous pangs from men that die:
So many plagues hath not the Apocalypse
As these wherewith they smite Thy friends ignored—
Even as I am; search my heart, and know;
My life, my sufferings bear Thy stamp and sign.
If Thou return to earth, come armed; for lo,
Thy foes prepare fresh crosses for Thee, Lord!
Not Turks, not Jews, but they who call them Thine.

XVIII.

TO DEATH.

Morte, stipendio della colpa.

O Death, the wage of our first father's blame,
Daughter of envy and nonentity,
Serf of the serpent, and his harlotry,
Thou beast most arrogant and void of shame!
Thy last great conquest dost thou dare proclaim,
Crying that all things are subdued to thee,
Against the Almighty raised almightily?—
The proofs that prop thy pride of state are lame.
Not to serve thee, but to make thee serve Him,
He stoops to Hell. The choice of arms was thine;
Yet art thou scoffed at by the crucified!

He lives—thy loss. He dies—from every limb,
   Mangled by thee, lightnings of godhead shine,
   From which thy darkness hath not where to hide.
XIX.

ON THE SEPULCHRE OF CHRIST.

No. I.

O tu ch' ami la parte.

O you who love the part more than the whole,
   And love yourself more than all human kind,
   Who persecute good men with prudence blind
   Because they combat your malign control,
See Scribes and Pharisees, each impious school,
   Each sect profane, o'erthrown by his great mind,
   Whose best our good to Deity refined,
   The while they thought Death triumphed o'er his soul.
Deem you that only you have thought and sense,
   While heaven and all its wonders, sun and earth,
   Scorned in your dullness, lack intelligence?
Fool! what produced you? These things gave you birth:
   So have they mind and God. Repent; be wise!
   Man fights but ill with Him who rules the skies.
XX.

ON THE SEPULCHRE OF CHRIST.

No. 2.

Quinci impara a stupirti.

Here bend in boundless wonder; bow your head:
   Think how God's deathless Mind, that men might be
   Robed in celestial immortality
   (O Love divine!), in flesh was raimented:
How He was killed and buried; from the dead
   How He arose to life with victory,
   And reigned in heaven; how all of us shall be
   Glorious like Him whose hearts to His are wed:
How they who die for love of reason, give
   Hypocrites, tyrants, sophists—all who sell
   Their neighbours ill for holiness—to hell:
How the dead saint condemns the bad who live;
   How all he does becomes a law for men;
   How he at last to judge shall come again!
XXI.

THE RESURRECTION.

Se sol sei ore.

If Christ was only six hours crucified
After few years of toil and misery,
Which for mankind He suffered willingly,
While heaven was won for ever when He died;
Why should He still be shown on every side,
Painted and preached, in nought but agony,
Whose pains were light matched with His victory,
When the world's power to harm Him was defied?
Why rather speak and write not of the realm
He rules in heaven, and soon will bring below
Unto the praise and glory of His name?
Ah foolish crowd! This world's thick vapours whelm
Your eyes unworthy of that glorious show,
Blind to His splendour, bent upon His shame.

XXII.

IDEAL LOVE.

Il vero amante.

He who loves truly, grows in force and might;
For beauty and the image of his love
Expand his spirit: whence he burns to prove
Adventures high, and holds all perils light.
If thus a lady's love dilate the knight,
What glories and what joy all joys above
Shall not the heavenly splendour, joined by love
Unto our flesh-imprisoned soul, excite?
Once freed, she would become one sphere immense
Of love, power, wisdom, filled with Deity,
Elate with wonders of the eternal Sense.
But we like sheep and wolves war ceaselessly:
That love we never seek, that light intense,
Which would exalt us to infinity.

XXIII.

THE MODERN CUPID.

Son tremil' anni.

Through full three thousand years the world reveres
Blind Love that bears the quiver and hath wings:
Now too he's deaf, and to the sufferings
Of folk in anguish turns impiteous ears.
Of gold he's greedy, and dark raiment wears;

A child no more, that naked sports and sings,
But a sly greybeard; no gold shaft he flings,
Now that fire-arms have cursed these latter years.
Charcoal and sulphur, thunder, lead, and smoke,
That leave the flesh with plagues of hell diseased,
And drive the craving spirit deaf and blind,
These are his weapons. But my bell hath broke
Her silence. Yield, thou deaf, blind, tainted beast,
To the wise fervour of a blameless mind!

XXIV.

TRUE AND FALSE NOBILITY.

In noi dal senno.

Valour and mind form real nobility,
The which bears fruit and shows a fair increase
By doughty actions: these and nought but these
Confer true patents of gentility.
Money is false and light unless it be
Bought by a man's own worthy qualities;
And blood is such that its corrupt disease
And ignorant pretence are foul to see.
Honours that ought to yield more true a type,
Europe, thou measurest by fortune still,
To thy great hurt; and this thy foe perceives:
He rates the tree by fruits mature and ripe,
Not by mere shadows, roots, and verdant leaves:—
Why then neglect so grave a cause of ill?

XXV.

THE PEOPLE.

Il popolo è una bestia.

The people is a beast of muddy brain,
That knows not its own force, and therefore stands
Loaded with wood and stone; the powerless hands
Of a mere child guide it with bit and rein:
One kick would be enough to break the chain;
But the beast fears, and what the child demands,
It does; nor its own terror understands,
Confused and stupefied by bugbears vain.
Most wonderful! with its own hand it ties
And gags itself—gives itself death and war
For pence doled out by kings from its own store.
Its own are all things between earth and heaven;
But this it knows not; and if one arise
To tell this truth, it kills him unforgiven.

XXVI.

CONSCIENCE.

Seco ogni coif a è doglia.

All crime is its own torment, bearing woe
   To mind or body or decrease of fame;
   If not at once, still step by step our name
   Or blood or friends or fortune it brings low.
But if our will do not resent the blow,
   We have not sinned. That penance hath no blame
   Which Magdalen found sweet: purging our shame,
   Self-punishment is virtue, all men know.
The consciousness of goodness pure and whole
   Makes a man fully blest; but misery
   Springs from false conscience, blinded in its pride.
This Simon Peter meant when he replied
   To Simon Magus, that the prescient soul
   Hath her own proof of immortality.

XXVII.

THE BAD PRINCE.

Mentola al comun corpo.

Organ of rut, not reason, is the lord
   Who from the body politic doth drain
   Lust for himself, instead of toil and pain,
   Leaving us lean as crickets on dry sward.
Well too if he like Love would filch our hoard
   With pleasure to ourselves, sluicing our vein
   And vigour to perpetuate the strain
   Of life by spilth of life within us stored!
Love's cheat yields joy and profit. Kings, less kind,
   Harm those they hoodwink; sow bare rock with seed;
   Nor use our waste to propagate the breed.
Heaven help that body which a little mind,
   Housed in a head, lacking ears, tongue, and eyes,
   And senseless but for smell, can tyrannise!

XXVIII.

ON ITALY.

La gran Donna.

That Lady who to Caesar came in state
   Upon the Rubicon, what time she feared
   Ruin from those strange races who appeared

Erewhile to build her empire strong and great,
Now stays with limbs dispersed and lacerate,
A bondslave, shorn of all her pomp revered:
Nor seems it now that Dinah's shame can gird
Simeon or Levi to avenge her fate.
If then Jerusalem doth not repair
To Nazareth or Athens, where did reign
Wisdom of God or man in days of yore,
None shall arise her honours to restore:
For Herods are all strangers; when they swear
To save the Saviour's seed, their oath is vain.

XXIX.

TO VENICE.

Nuova arca di Noè.

New Ark of Noah! when the cruel scourge
Of that barbarian tyrant like a wave
Went over Italy, thou then didst save
The seed of just men on the weltering surge.
Here, still by discord and foul servitude
Untainted, thou a hero brood dost raise,
Powerful and prudent. Due to thee their praise
Of maiden pure, of teeming motherhood!
Thou wonder of the world, Rome's loyal heir,
Thou pride and strong support of Italy,
Dial of princes, school of all things wise!
Thou like Arcturus steadfast in the skies,
With tardy sense guidest thy kingdom fair,
Bearing alone the load of liberty.

XXX.

TO GENOA.

Le Ninfe d'Arno.

The nymphs of Arno; Adria's goddess-queen;
Greece, where the Latin banner floated free;
The lands that border on the Syrian sea;
The Euxine, and fair Naples; these have been
Thine, by the right of conquest; these should be
Still thine by empire: Asia's broad demesne,
Afric, America—realms never seen
But by thy venture—all belong to thee.
But thou, thyself not knowing, leavest all
For a poor price to strangers; since thy head
Is weak, albeit thy limbs are stout and good.
Genoa, mistress of the world, recall

Thy soul magnanimous! Nay, be not led
Slave to base gold, thou and thy tameless brood!

XXXI.

TO POLAND.

Sopra i regni.

High o'er those realms that make blind chance the heir
Of empire, Poland, dost thou lift thy head:
For while thou mournest for thy monarch dead,
Thou wilt not let his son the sceptre bear,
Lest he prove weak perchance to do or dare.
Yet art thou even more by luck misled,
Choosing a prince of fortune, courtly-bred,
Uncertain whether he will spend or spare.
Oh, quit this pride! In hut or shepherd's pen
Seek Cato, Minos, Numa! For of such
God still makes kings in plenty: and these men
Will squander little substance and gain much,
Knowing that virtue and not blood shall be
Their titles to true immortality.

XXXII.

TO THE SWISS.

Se voi più innalza.

Ye Alpine rocks! If less your peaks elate
To heaven exalt you than that gift divine,
Freedom; why do your children still combine
To keep the despots in their stolen state?
Lo, for a piece of bread from windows wide
You fling your blood, taking no thought what cause,
Righteous or wrong, your strength to battle draws;
So is your valour spurned and vilified.
All things belong to free men; but the slave
Clothes and feeds poorly. Even so from you
Broad lands and Malta's knighthood men withhold.
Up, free yourselves, and act as heroes do!
Go, take your own from tyrants, which you gave
So recklessly, and they so dear have sold!

XXXIII.

THE SAMARITAN.

Da Roma ad Ostia.

From Rome to Ostia a poor man went;

Thieves robbed and wounded him upon the way;
Some monks, great saints, observed him where he lay,
And left him, on their breviaries intent.
A Bishop passed thereby, and careless bent
To sign the cross, a blessing brief to say;
But a great Cardinal, to clutch their prey,
Followed the thieves, falsely benevolent.
At last there came a German Lutheran,
Who builds on faith, merit of works withstands;
He raised and clothed and healed the dying man.
Now which of these was worthiest, most humane?
The heart is better than the head, kind hands
Than cold lip-service; faith without works is vain.
Who understands
What creed is good and true for self and others?—
But none can doubt the good he doth his brothers.

XXXIV.

HYPOCRITES.

Nessun ti venne a dir.

Who comes and saith: 'A Tyrant, lo, am I!'
And, 'I am Antichrist!' what man will swear?
The crafty rogue, hiding his poisonous ware,
Sells you what slays your soul, for sanctity.
Cheats, brigands, prostitutes, and all that fry,
Not having fashioned so devout a snare,
Appear worse sinners than perhaps they are;
For where the craft's small, small's the villainy;
You're on your guard. The meek Samaritan
Makes way before those guileful Pharisees,
Though God assigned to him the higher place.
Not words nor wonders prove a virtuous man,
But deeds and acts. How many deities
Hath this false standard given the human race!

XXXV.

SOPHISTS.

Nessun ti verrà a dire.

'Behold, I am a Sophist!' no man saith.
But the true sons of perfidy refined
Forge theologic lies the soul to blind,
Calling themselves evangels of the faith.
Aretine with his scoundrels blew his breath,
And in the cynic orgies boldly joined;
His ribald jests had flowers and thorns combined—

A frank fair list including life and death,
For fun, not fraud. It shames him to be found
Less vile than those who cannot bear to see
Their sink of filth laid open to the ground:
Wherefore they shut our mouths, our books impound,
Garble with lies each sentence that may be
Cited to prove their foul hypocrisy.

XXXVI.

AGAINST HYPOCRITES.

Gli affetti di Pluton.

Deep in their hearts they hide the lusts of Hell:
Christ's name is written on their brow, that those
Who only view the husk, may not suppose
What guile and malice harbour in the shell.
O God! O Wisdom! Holy Fervour! Well
Of strength invincible to strike Thy foes!
Give me the force—my spirit burns and glows—
To strip those idols and to break their spell!
The zeal I bear unto Thy name benign,
The love I feel for truth sincere and pure,
When such men triumph, make me rend my hair.
How long shall folk this infamy endure—
That he should be held sacred, he divine,
Who strips e'en corpses in the graveyard bare?

XXXVII.

ON THE LORD'S PRAYER.

No. I.

Vilissima progenie.

Ye vile offscourings! with unblushing face
Dare ye claim sonship to our heavenly Sire,
Who serve brute vices, crouching in the mire
To hounds and conies, beasts that ape our race?
Such truckling is called virtue by the base
Hucksters of sophistry, the priest and friar,—
Gilt claws of tyrant brutes,—who lie for hire,
Preaching that God delights in this disgrace.
Look well, ye brainless folk! Do fathers hold
Their children slaves to serfs? Do sheep obey
The witless ram? Why make a beast your king?
If there are no archangels, let your fold
Be governed by the sense of all: why stray
From men to worship every filthy thing?

XXXVIII.

ON THE LORD'S PRAYER.

No. 2.

Dov' è la libertà.

Where are the freedom and high feats that spring
   From fatherhood so fair as Deity?
   Fleas are no sons of men, although they be
   Flesh-born: brave thoughts and deeds this honour bring.
If princes great or small seek anything
   Adverse to good and God's authority,
   Which of you dares refuse? Nay, who is he
   That doth not cringe to do their pleasuring?
So then with soul and blood in verity
   You serve base gold, vices, and worthless men—
   God with lip-service only and with lies,
Sunk in the slough of dire idolatry:
   If Ignorance begat these errors, then
   To Reason turn for sonship and be wise!

XXXIX.

ON THE LORD'S PRAYER.

No. 3.

Allor potrete orar.

Then shall ye pray with every hour that flies;
   Thy kingdom come, and let Thy will be done
   On earth as in the spheres above the sun,
   When all we hoped and wished shall bless our eyes.
Poets shall see their Age of Gold arise,
   Fairer than feigned in hymn or orison;
   Yea, all the realm by Adam's sin undone
   Shall be restored in sinless Paradise.
Philosophers shall govern for their own
   That perfect commonwealth whereof they write,
   The which on earth as yet was never known.
Judah to Sion shall return with might
   Of greater wonders than shook Pharaoh's throne,
   From Babylon, to bless the prophets' sight.

XL.

A PROPHECY OF JUDGMENT.

No. 1.

THE REIGN OF ANTICHRIST.

Mentre l'acquila invola.

While yet the eagle preys, and growls the bear;
While roars the lion; while the crow defies
The lamb who raised our race above the skies;
While yet the dove laments to the deaf air;
While, mixed with goodly wheat, darnel and tare
Within the field of human nature rise;—
Let that ungodly sect, profanely wise,
That scorns our hope, feed, fatten, and beware!
Soon comes the day when those grim giants fell,
Famed through the world, dyed deep with sanguine hue,
Whom with feigned flatteries you applaud, shall be
Swept from the earth, and sunk in horrid Hell,
Girt round with flames, to weep and wail with you,
In doleful dungeons everlastingly.

XLI.

A PROPHECY OF JUDGMENT.

No. 2.

THE DOOM OF THE IMPIOUS.

La scuola inimicissima.

You sect most adverse to the good and true,
Degenerate from your origin divine,
Pastured on lies and shadows by the line
Of Thais, Sinon, Judas, Homer! You,
Thus saith the Spirit, when the retinue
Of saints with Christ returns on earth to shine,
When the fifth angel's vial pours condign
Vengeance with awful ire and torments due,—
You shall be girt with gloom; your lips profane,
Disloyal tongues, and savage teeth shall grind
And gnash with fury fell and anger vain:
In Malebolge your damned souls confined
On fiery marle, for increment of pain,
Shall see the saved rejoice with mirth of mind.

XLII.

A PROPHECY OF JUDGMENT.

No. 3.

THE GOLDEN AGE.

Se fu nel mondo.

If men were happy in that age of gold,
We yet may hope to see mild Saturn's reign;
For all things that were buried live again,
By time's revolving cycle forward rolled.
Yet this the fox, the wolf, the crow, made bold
By fraud and perfidy, deny—in vain:
For God that rules, the signs in heaven, the train
Of prophets, and all hearts this faith uphold.
If thine and mine were banished in good sooth
From honour, pleasure, and utility,
The world would turn, I ween, to Paradise;
Blind love to modest love with open eyes;
Cunning and ignorance to living truth;
And foul oppression to fraternity.

XLIII.

THE MILLENNIUM.

Non piaccia a Dio.

Nay, God forbid that mid these tragic throes
To idle comedy my thought should bend,
When torments dire and warning woes portend
Of this our world the instantaneous close!
The day approaches which shall discompose
All earthly sects, the elements shall blend
In utter ruin, and with joy shall send
Just spirits to their spheres in heaven's repose.
The Highest comes in Holy Land to hold
His sovran court and synod sanctified,
As all the psalms and prophets have foretold:
The riches of his grace He will spread wide
Through his own realm, that seat and chosen fold
Of worship and free mercies multiplied.

XLIV.

THE PRESENT.

Convien al secol nostro.

Black robes befit our age. Once they were white;
Next many-hued; now dark as Afric's Moor,
Night-black, infernal, traitorous, obscure,
Horrid with ignorance and sick with fright.
For very shame we shun all colours bright,

Who mourn our end—the tyrants we endure,
The chains, the noose, the lead, the snares, the lure—
Our dismal heroes, our souls sunk in night.
Black weeds again denote that extreme folly
Which makes us blind, mournful, and woe-begone:
For dusk is dear to doleful melancholy;
Nathless fate's wheel still turns: this raiment dun
We shall exchange hereafter for the holy
Garments of white in which of yore we shone.

XLV.

THE FUTURE.

Veggo in candida robba.

Clothed in white robes I see the Holy Sire
Descend to hold his court amid the band
Of shining saints and elders: at his hand
The white immortal Lamb commands their choir.
John ends his long lament for torments dire,
Now Judah's lion rises to expand
The fatal book, and the first broken band
Sends the white courier forth to work God's ire.
The first fair spirits raimented in white
Go out to meet him who on his white cloud
Comes heralded by horsemen white as snow.
Ye black-stoled folk, be dumb, who hate the loud
Blare of God's lifted angel-trumpets! Lo,
The pure white dove puts the black crows to flight!

XLVI.

THE YEAR 1603.

Già sto mirando.

The first heaven-wandering lights I see ascend
Upon the seventh and ninth centenary,
When in the Archer's realm three years shall be
Added, this aeon and our age to end.
Thou too, Mercurius, like a scribe dost lend
Thine aid to promulgate that dread decree,
Stored in the archives of eternity,
And signed and sealed by powers no prayers can bend.
O'er Europe's full meridian on thy morn
In the tenth house thy court I see thee hold:
The Sun with thee consents in Capricorn.
God grant that I may keep this mortal breath
Until I too that glorious day behold
Which shall at last confound the sons of death!

XLVII.

NEBUCHADNEZZAR'S IMAGE.

Babel disfatta.

The golden head was Babylon; she passed:
   Persia came next, the silvern breast: whereto
   Joined brazen flank and belly—these are you,
   Ye men of Macedon! Now Rome's the last.
Rome on two iron legs towered tall and vast;
   But at her feet were toes of clay, that drew
   Downfall: those scattered tribes erewhile she knew
   For lords; now 'neath her fatal sway they're cast.
Ah thirsty soil! From your parched fallow fumes
   A smoke of pride, vain-glory, cruelty,
   That blinds, infects, and blackens, and consumes!
To Daniel, to the Bible you refuse
   Your rebel sense; for it is still your use
   To screen yourself with lies and sophistry.

XLVIII.

THE DUNGEON.

Come va al centro.

As to the centre all things that have weight
   Sink from the surface: as the silly mouse
   Runs at a venture, rash though timorous,
   Into the monster's jaws to meet her fate:
Thus all who love high Science, from the strait
   Dead sea of Sophistry sailing like us
   Into Truth's ocean, bold and amorous,
   Must in our haven anchor soon or late.
One calls this haunt a Cave of Polypheme,
   And one Atlante's Palace, one of Crete
   The Labyrinth, and one Hell's lowest pit.
Knowledge, grace, mercy, are an idle dream
   In this dread place. Nought but fear dwells in it,
   Of stealthy Tyranny the sacred seat.

XLIX.

THE SAGE ON EARTH.

Sciolto e legato.

Bound and yet free, companioned and alone,
   Loud mid my silence, I confound my foes:
   Men think me fool in this vile world of woes;

God's wisdom greets me sage from heaven's high throne.
With wings on earth oppressed aloft I bound;
My gleeful soul sad bonds of flesh enclose:
And though sometimes too great the burden grows,
These pinions bear me upward from the ground.
A doubtful combat proves the warrior's might:
Short is all time matched with eternity:
Nought than a pleasing burden is more light.
My brows I bind with my love's effigy,
Sure that my joyous flight will soon be sped
Where without speech my thoughts shall all be read.

L.

THE PRICE OF FREEDOM.

D' Italia in Grecia.

From Rome to Greece, from Greece to Libya's sand,
Yearning for liberty, just Cato went;
Nor finding freedom to his heart's content,
Sought it in death, and died by his own hand.
Wise Hannibal, when neither sea nor land
Could save him from the Roman eagles, rent
His soul with poison from imprisonment;
And a snake's tooth cut Cleopatra's band.
In this way died one valiant Maccabee;
Brutus feigned madness; prudent Solon hid
His sense; and David, when he feared Gath's king.
Thus when the Mystic found that Jonah's sea
Was yawning to engulf him, what he did
He gave to God—a wise man's offering.

LI.

APOLOGY BY PARADOX.

Non é brutto il Demon.

The Devil's not so ugly as they paint;
He's well with all, compact of courtesy:
Real heroism is real piety:
Before small truth great falsehoods shrink and faint
If pots stain worse than pipkins, it were quaint
To charge the pipkins with impurity:
Freedom I crave: who craves not to be free?
Yet life that must be feigned for, leaves a taint.
Ill conduct brings repentance?—If you prate
This wise to me, why prate not thus to all
Philosophers and prophets, and to Christ?
Not too much learning, as some arrogate,

But the small brains of dullards have sufficed
To make us wretched and the world enthrall.

LII.

THE SOUL'S APOLOGY.

Ben sei mila anni.

Six thousand years or more on earth I've been:
Witness those histories of nations dead,
Which for our age I have illustrated
In philosophic volumes, scene by scene.
And thou, mere mite, seeing my sun serene
Eclipsed, wilt argue that I had no head
To live by.—Why not try the sun instead,
If nought in fate unfathomed thou hast seen?
If wise men, whom the world rebukes, combined
With tyrant wolves, brute beasts we should become.
The sage, once stoned for sin, you canonise.
When rennet melts, much milk makes haste to bind.
The more you blow the flames, the more they rise,
Bloom into stars, and find in heaven their home.

LIII.

TO GOD ON PRAYER.

Tu che Forza ed Amor.

O Thou, who, mingling Force and Love, dost draw
And guide the complex of all entities,
Framed for that purpose; whence our reason sees
In supreme Fate the synthesis of Law;
Though prayers transgress which find defect or flaw
In things foredoomed by Thy divine decrees,
Yet wilt Thou modify, by slow degrees
Or swift, good times or bad Thy mind foresaw:
I therefore pray—I who through years have been
The scorn of fools, the butt of impious men,
Suffering new pains and torments day by day—
Shorten this anguish, Lord, these griefs allay;
For still Thou shalt not have changed counsel when
I soar from hence to liberty foreseen.

LIV.

TO GOD FOR HELP.

Come vuoi, ch' a buon porto.

How wilt Thou I should gain a harbour fair,

If after proof among my friends I find
That some are faithless, some devoid of mind,
Some short of sense, though stout to do and dare?
If some, though wise and loyal, like the hare
Hide in a hole, or fly in terror blind,
While nerve with wisdom and with faith combined
Through malice and through penury despair?
Reason, Thy honour, and my weal eschewed
That false ally who said he came from Thee,
With promise vain of power and liberty.
I trust:—I'll do. Change Thou the bad to good!—
But ere I raise me to that altitude,
Needs must I merge in Thee as Thou in me.
LV.

To Annibale Caraccioli,

A WRITER OF ECLOGUES.

Non Licida, nè Driope.

Lycoris, Lycidas, and Dryope
Cannot, dear Niblo, save thy name from death;
Shadows that fleet, and flowers that yield their breath,
Match not the Love that craves infinity.
The beauty thou dost worship dwells in thee:
Within thy soul divine it harboureth:
This also bids my spirit soar, and saith
Words that unsphere for me heaven's harmony.
Make then thine inborn lustre beam and shine
With love of goodness; goodness cannot fail:
From God alone let praise immense be thine.
My soul is tired of telling o'er the tale
With men: she calls on thine: she bids thee go
Into God's school with tablets white as snow.
LVI.

TO TELESIUS OF COSENZA.

Telesio, il telo.

Telesius, the arrow from thy bow
Midmost his band of sophists slays that high
Tyrant of souls that think; he cannot fly:
While Truth soars free, loosed by the self-same blow.
Proud lyres with thine immortal praises glow,
Smitten by bards elate with victory:
Lo, thine own Cavalcante, stormfully
Lightning, still strikes the fortress of the foe!

Good Gaieta bedecks our saint serene
   With robes translucent, light-irradiate,
   Restoring her to all her natural sheen;
The while my tocsin at the temple-gate
   Of the wide universe proclaims her queen,
   Pythia of first and last ordained by fate.

LVII.

TO RIDOLFO DI BINA.

Senno ed Amor.

Wisdom and love, O Bina, gave thee wings,
   Before the blossom of thy years had faded,
   To fly with Adam for thy guide, God-aided,
   Through many lands in divers journeyings.
Pure virtue is thy guerdon: virtue brings
   Glory to thee, death to the foes degraded,
   Who through long years of darkness have invaded
   Thy Germany, mother of slaves not kings.
Yet, gazing on heaven's book, heroic child,
   My soul discerns graces divine in thee:—
   Leave toys and playthings to the crowd of fools!
Do thou with heart fervent and proudly mild
   Make war upon those fraud-engendering schools!
   I see thee victor, and in God I see.

LVIII.

TO TOBIA ADAMI.

Portando in man.

Holding the cynic lantern in your hand,
   Through Europe, Egypt, Asia, you have passed,
   Till at Ausonia's feet you find at last
   That Cyclops' cave, where I, to darkness banned,
In light eternal forge for you the brand
   Against Abaddon, who hath overcast
   The truth and right, Adami, made full fast
   Unto God's glory by our steadfast band.
Go, smite each sophist, tyrant, hypocrite!
   Girt with the arms of the first Wisdom, free
   Your country from the frauds that cumber it!
Swerve not: 'twere sin. How good, how great the praise
   Of him who turns youth, strength, soul, energy,
   Unto the dayspring of the eternal rays!

LIX.

A SONNET ON CAUCASUS.

Temo che per morir.

I fear that by my death the human race
Would gain no vantage. Thus I do not die.
So wide is this vast cage of misery
That flight and change lead to no happier place.
Shifting our pains, we risk a sorrier case:
All worlds, like ours, are sunk in agony:
Go where we will, we feel; and this my cry
I may forget like many an old disgrace.
Who knows what doom is mine? The Omnipotent
Keeps silence; nay, I know not whether strife
Or peace was with me in some earlier life.
Philip in a worse prison me hath pent
These three days past—but not without God's will.
Stay we as God decrees: God doth no ill.

LX.

GOD MADE AND GOD RULES.

La fabbrica del mondo.

The fabric of the world—earth, air, and skies—
Each particle thereof and tiniest part
Designed for special ends—proclaims the art
Of an almighty Maker good and wise.
Nathless the lawless brutes, our crimes and lies,
The joys of vicious men, the good man's smart,
All creatures swerving from their ends, impart
Doubts that the Ruler is nor good nor wise.
Can it then be that boundless Power, Love, Mind,
Lets others reign, the while He takes repose?
Hath He grown old, or hath He ceased to heed?
Nay, one God made and rules: He shall unwind
The tangled skein; the hidden law disclose,
Whereby so many sinned in thought and deed.

NOTES ON MICHAEL ANGELO'S SONNETS.

I. Quoted by Donato Giannotti in his Dialogue De' giorni che Dante consumò nel cercare l'Inferno e 'l Purgatorio. The date of its composition is perhaps 1545.

II. Written probably for Donato Giannotti about the same date.

III. Belonging to the year 1506, when Michael Angelo quarrelled with Julius and left Rome in anger. The tree referred to in the last line is the oak of the Rovere family.

IV. Same date, and same circumstances. The autograph has these words at the foot of the sonnet: Vostro Miccelangniolo, in Turchia. Rome itself, the Sacred City, has become a land of infidels.

V. Ser Giovanni da Pistoja was Chancellor of the Florentine Academy. The date is probably 1509. The Sonetto a Coda is generally humorous or satiric.

VI. Written in one of those moments of affanno or stizzo to which the sculptor was subject. For the old bitterness of feeling between Florence and Pistoja, see Dante, Inferno.

VII. Michael Angelo was ill during the summer of 1544, and was nursed by Luigi del Riccio in his own house, Shortly after his recovery he quarrelled with his friend, and wrote him this sonnet as well as a very angry letter.

VIII. p. 38. Cecchino Bracci was a boy of rare and surpassing beauty who died at Rome, January 8, 1544, in his seventeenth year. Besides this sonnet, which refers to a portrait Luigi del Riccio had asked him to make of the dead youth, Michael Angelo composed a series of forty-eight quatrains upon the same subject, and sent them to his friend Luigi. Michelangelo the younger, thinking that 'l'ignoranzia degli uomini ha campo di mormorare,' suppressed the name Cecchino and changed lui into lei. Date about 1544.

IX. Line 4: 'The Archangel's scales alone can weigh my gratitude against your gift.' Lines 5-8: 'Your courtesy has taken away all my power of responding to it. I am as helpless as a ship becalmed, or a wisp of straw on a stormy sea.'

X. Michael Angelo, when asked to make a portrait of his friend's mistress, declares that he is unable to do justice to her beauty. The name Mancina is a pun upon the Italian word for the left arm, Mancino. This lady was a famous and venal beauty, mentioned among the loves of the poet Molsa.

XI. Date, 1550.

XII. This and the three next sonnets may with tolerable certainty be referred to the series written on various occasions for Vittoria Colonna.

XIII. Sent together with a letter, in which we read: l'aportatore di questa sarà Urbino, che sta meco. Urbino was M. A.'s old servant, workman, and friend. See No. LXVIII. and note.

XIV. The thought is that, as the sculptor carves a statue from a rough model by addition and subtraction of the marble, so the lady of his heart refines and perfects his rude native character.

XV. This sonnet is the theme of Varchi's Lezione. There is nothing to prove that it was addressed to Vittoria Colonna. Varchi calls it 'un suo altissimo sonetto pieno di quella antica purezza e dantesca gravità.'

XVI. The thought of the fifteenth is repeated with some variations. His lady's heart holds for the lover good and evil things, according as he has the art to draw them forth.

XVIII. In the terzets he describes the temptations of the artist-nature, over-sensitive to beauty. Michelangelo the younger so altered these six lines as to destroy the autobiographical allusion.—Cp. No. XXVIII., note.

XIX. The lover's heart is like an intaglio, precious by being inscribed with his lady's image.

XX. An early composition, written on the back of a letter sent to the sculptor in Bologna by his brother Simone in 1507. M.A. was then working at the bronze statue of Julius II. Who the lady of his love was, we do not know. Notice the absence of Platonic concetti.

XXIII. It is hardly necessary to call attention to Michael Angelo's oft-recurring Platonism. The thought that the eye alone perceives the celestial beauty, veiled beneath the fleshly form of the beloved, is repeated in many sonnets—especially in XXV., XXVIII.

XXIV. Composed probably in the year 1529.

XXV. Written on the same sheet as the foregoing sonnet, and composed probably in the same year. The thought is this: beauty passing from the lady into the lover's soul, is there spiritualised and becomes the object of a spiritual love.

XXVII. To escape from his lady, either by interposing another image of beauty between the thought of her and his heart, or by flight, is impossible.

XXVIII. Compare Madrigal VII. in illustration of lines 5 to 8. By the analogy of that passage, I should venture to render lines 6 and 7 thus:

He made thee light, and me the eyes of art;
Nor fails my soul to find God's counterpart.

XXX. Varchi, quoting this sonnet in his Lezione, conjectures that it was composed for Tommaso Cavalieri.

XXXI. Varchi asserts without qualification that this sonnet was addressed to Tommaso Cavalieri. The pun in the last line, Resto prigion d'un Cavalier armato, seems to me to decide the matter, though Signor Guasti and Signor Gotti both will have it that a woman must have been intended. Michelangelo the younger has only left one line, the second, untouched in his rifacimento. Instead of the last words he gives un cuor di virtù armato, being over-scrupulous for his great-uncle's reputation.

XXXII. Written at the foot of a letter addressed by Giuliano Bugiardini the painter, from Florence, to M.A. in Rome, August 5, 1532. This then is probably the date of the composition.

XXXIV. The metaphor of fire, flint, and mortar breaks down in the last line, where M.A. forgets that gold cannot strike a spark from stone.

XXXV. Line 9 has the word Signor. It is almost certain that where M.A. uses this word without further qualification in a love sonnet, he means his mistress. I have sometimes translated it 'heart's lord' or 'loved lord,' because I did not wish to merge the quaintness of this ancient Tuscan usage in the more commonplace 'lady.'

XXXVI. Line 3: the lord, etc. This again is the poet's mistress. The drift of the sonnet is this: his soul can find no expression but through speech, and speech is too gross to utter the purity of his feeling. His mistress again receives his tongue's message with her ears; and thus there is an element of sensuality, false and alien to his intention, both in his complaint and in her acceptation of it. The last line is a version of the proverb: chi è avvezzo a dir bugie, non crede a nessuno.

XXXVII. At the foot of the sonnet is written Mandato. The two last lines play on the words signor and signoria. To whom it was sent we do not know for certain; but we may conjecture Vittoria Colonna.

XXXIX. The paper on which this sonnet is written has a memorandum with the date January 6, 1529. 'On my return from Venice, I, Michelagniolo Buonarroti, found in the house about five loads of straw,' etc. It belongs therefore to the period of the siege of Florence, when M.A., as is well known, fled for a short space to Venice. In line 12, I have translated il mie signiore, my lady.

XL. No sonnet in the whole collection seems to have cost M.A. so much trouble as this. Besides the two completed versions, which I have rendered, there are several scores of rejected or various readings for single lines in the MSS. The Platonic doctrine of Anamnesis probably supplies the key to the thought which the poet attempted to work out.

XLI., XLII., XLIII., XLIV. There is nothing to prove that these four sonnets on Night were composed in sequence. On the contrary, the personal tone of XLI. seems to separate this from the other three. XLIV. may be accepted as a palinode for XLIII.

XLV., XLVI. Both sonnets deal half humorously with a thought very prominent in M.A.'s compositions—the effect of love on one who is old in years. Cp. XLVIII., L.

XLVII. The Platonic conception that the pure form of Beauty or of Truth, if seen, would be overwhelming in its brilliancy.

XLIX. The dolcie pianto and eterna pace are the tears and peace of piety. The doloroso riso and corta pace are the smiles and happiness of earthly love.

LII. Here is another version of this very beautiful sonnet.

No mortal thing enthralled these longing eyes
When perfect peace in thy fair face I found;
But far within, where all is holy ground,
My soul felt Love, her comrade of the skies:

For she was born with God in Paradise;
Nor all the shows of beauty shed around
This fair false world her wings to earth have bound;
Unto the Love of Loves aloft she flies.
Nay, things that suffer death, quench not the fire
Of deathless spirits; nor eternity
Serves sordid Time, that withers all things rare.
Not love but lawless impulse is desire:
That slays the soul; our love makes still more fair
Our friends on earth, fairer in death on high.

LIII. This is the doctrine of the Symposium; the scorn of merely sexual love is also Platonic.

LIV. Another sonnet on the theme of the Uranian as distinguished from the Vulgar love. See below, LVL., for a parallel to the second terzet.

LV. The date maybe 1532. The play on words in the first quatrain and the first terzet is Shakespearian.

LIX. Two notes, appended to the two autographs of this sonnet, show that M.A. regarded it as a jeu d'esprit, 'Per carnovale par lecito far qualche pazzia a chi non va in maschera.' 'Questo non è fuoco da carnovale, però vel mando di quaresima; e a voi mi rachomando. Vostro Michelagniolo.'

LXL. Date 1547. No sonnet presents more difficulties than this, in which M.A. has availed himself of a passage in the Cratylus of Plato. The divine hammer spoken of in the second couplet is the ideal pattern after which the souls of men are fashioned; and this in the first terzet seems to be identified with Vittoria Colonna. In the second terzet he regards his own soul as imperfect, lacking the final touches which it might have received from hers. See XIV. for a somewhat similar conceit.

LXIV. The image is that of a glowing wood coal smouldering away to embers amid its own ashes.

LXV. Date 1554. Addressed A messer Giorgio Vasari, amico e pittor singulare, with this letter: Messer Giorgio, amico caro, voi direte ben ch' io sie vecchio e pazzo a voler far sonetti; ma perchè molti dicono ch' io son rimbambito, ho voluto far l'uficio mio, ec. A dì 19 di settembre 1554. Vostro Michelagniolo Buonarroti in Roma.

LXVL, LXVII. These two sonnets were sent to Giorgio Vasari in 1555(?) with this letter: Messer Giorgio, io vi mando dua sonetti; e benchè sieno cosa sciocca, il fo perchè veggiate dove io tengo i mie' pensieri: e quando arete ottantuno anni, come ò io, mi crederete. Pregovi gli diate a messer Giovan Francesco Fattucci, che me ne à chiesti. Vostro Michelagniolo Buonarroti in Roma. The first was also sent to Monsignor Beccadelli, Archbishop of Ragusa, who replied to it. For his sonnet, see Signor Guasti's edition, p. 233.

LXVIII. Date 1556. Written in reply to his friend's invitation that he should pay him a visit at Ragusa. Line 10: this Urbino was M.A.'s old and faithful servant, Francesco d'Amadore di Casteldurante, who lived with him twenty-six years, and died at Rome in 1556.

LXIX.-LXXVII. The dates of this series of penitential sonnets are not known. It is clear that they were written in old age. It will be remembered that the latest piece of marble on which Michael Angelo worked, was the unfinished Pietà now standing behind the choir of the Duomo at Florence. Many of his latest drawings are designs for a Crucifixion.

NOTES ON CAMPANELLA'S SONNETS.

I. Line 1: the Italian words which I have translated God's Wisdom and Philosophy are Senno and Sofia. Campanella held that the divine Senno penetrated the whole universe, and, meeting with created Sofia, gave birth to Science. This sonnet is therefore a sort of Mythopoem, figuring the process whereby true knowledge, as distinguished from sophistry, is derived by the human reason interrogating God in Nature and within the soul. Line 5: Sofia has for her husband Senno; the human intellect is married to the divine. Line 9: it was the doctrine of Campanella and the school to which he belonged, that no advance in knowledge could be made except by the direct exploration of the universe, and that the authority of schoolmen, Aristotelians, and the like, must be broken down before a step could be made in the right direction. This germ of modern science is sufficiently familiar to us in the exposition of Bacon. Line 12: repeats the same idea. Facts presented by Nature are of more value than any Ipse dixit. Line 14: he compares himself not without reason to Prometheus; for twenty-five years spent in prison were his reward for the revelation which has added a new sphere to human thought.

II. The bitter words of this sonnet will not seem unmerited to those who have studied Italian poetry in the Cinque Cento—the refined playthings of verse, the romances, and the burlesque nonsense, which amused a corrupt though highly cultivated age.

III. Campanella held the doctrine of an Anima Mundi in the fullest and deepest sense of the term. The larger and more complex the organism, the more it held, in his opinion, of thought and sentient life. Thus the stars, in the language of Aristotle, are [Greek: thiotera aemon]. Compare Sonnets VIII., XIX.

IV. Though the material seat of the mind is so insignificant, the mind itself is infinite, analogous to God in its capacity. Aristarchus and Metrodorus symbolise, perhaps, the spheres of literature and mathematics. This infinitude of the intellect is our real proof of God, our inner witness of the Deity. We may arrive at God by reasoning; we may trust authority; but it is only by impregnating our minds with God in Nature that we come into immediate contact with Him. Cp. Sonnet VI., last line.

V. The theme of this sonnet is the well-known Baconian principle of the interrogation of Nature. The true philosopher must go straight to the universe, and not confine himself to books. Cp. Sonnets I., LV., LVI.

VI. A further development of the same thought. Tyrants, hypocrites, sophists are the three plagues of humanity, standing between our intellect and God, who is the source of freedom, goodness, and true wisdom. In the last line Campanella expresses his opinion that God is knowable by an immediate act of perception analogous to the sense of taste: Se tutti al Senno non rendiamo il gusto. Compare Sonnet IV., last line.

VII. Ignorance is the parent of tyranny, sophistry, hypocrisy; and the arms against this trinity of error are power, wisdom, love, the three main attributes of God.

VIII. Human egotism inclines men to deny the spiritual life of the universe, to favour their own nation, to love their individual selves exclusively, to eliminate the true God from the world, to worship false gods fashioned from them selves, and at last to fancy themselves central and creative in the Cosmos. Adami calls this sonnet scoprimento stupendo.

IX. The quatrains set forth the condition of the soul besotted with self love. We may see in this picture a critique of Machiavelli's Principe, which was for Campanella the very ideal portrait of a tyrant. The love of God, rightly understood, places man en rapport with all created things. S. Francis, for example, loved not only his fellow men, but recognised the brotherhood of birds and fishes.

X. Ignorance, the source of all our miseries, blinds us to celestial beauty and makes us follow carnal lust. Yet what is best in sexual love is the radiance of heavenly beauty shining through the form of flesh. This sonnet receives abundant illustration in Michael Angelo's poems.

XI, XII. Two sonnets on the condition of the philosopher in a world that understands him not. The first expresses that sense of inborn royalty which sustained Campanella through his long martyrdom. The second expands the picture drawn of the philosopher in Plato's Republic after his return to the cave from the region of truth.

XIII. Campanella frequently expressed his theological fatalism by this metaphor of a comedy. God wrote the drama which men have to play. In this life we cannot understand our parts. We act what is appointed for us, and it is only when the comedy is finished, that we shall see how good and evil, happiness and misery, were all needed by the great life of the universe. The following stanza from one of his Canzoni may be cited in illustration:

War, ignorance, fraud, tyranny,
Death, homicide, abortion, woe—
These to the world are fair, as we
Reckon the chase or gladiatorial show
To pile our hearth we fell the tree,
Kill bird or beast our strength to stay,
The vines, the hives our wants obey—
Like spiders spreading nets, we take and slay
As tragedy gives men delight,
So the exchange of death and strife
Still yields a pleasure infinite
To the great world's triumphant life
Nay seeming ugliness and pain
Avert returning Chaos' reign—
Thus the whole world's a comedy,

And they who by philosophy
Unite themselves to God, will see
In ugliness and evil nought
But beauteous masks—oh, mirthful thought!

XIV. The same theme is continued with a further development. Men among themselves play their own comedy, but do not rightly assign the parts. They make kings of slavish souls, and elevate the impious to the rank of saints. They ignore their true and natural leaders, and stone the real prophets.

XV. Between the false kings of men, who owe their thrones to accident, and the really royal, who by chance of birth or station are a prey to tyrants, there is everlasting war. Yet the spirit of the martyrs survives, and long after their death they rule.

XVI. True kinghood is independent of royal birth or power or ensigns. High moral and intellectual qualities make the natural kings of men, and these are so rarely found in sceptred families that a republic is the safest form of government. See Sonnets XXXI., XXXVII.

XVII. As men mistake their kings, so they mistake the saints. The true spirit of Christ is ignored, and if Christ were to return to earth, they would persecute him, even as they persecute those who follow him most closely in their lives and doctrines.

XVIII. Christ symbolises and includes all saintly truth-seeking souls. Compare the three last lines of this sonnet with the three last lines of No. XV. and No. XX.

XIX., XX., XXI. Expanding the same themes, Campanella contrasts the ignorance of self-love with the divine illumination of the true philosopher, and insists that, in spite of persecution and martyrdom, saintly and truth-seeking souls will triumph.

XXII. Resumes the thought of No. X. If only the soul of man, infinite in its capacity, could be enamoured of God, it would at once work miracles and attain to Deity.

XXIII. A bitter satire on love in the seventeenth century. Lines 9-11: as Adami sometimes says, qui legit intelligat. Line 12: la squilla mia is a pun on Campanella's name. He means that he has shown the world a more excellent way of love. Cp. No. XXII.

XXIV. The essence of nobility is subjected to the same critique as kinghood in No. XVI. Line 11: the Turk is Europe's foe. Campanella praises the Turks because they had no hereditary nobility, and conferred honours on men according to their actions.

XXV. That this sonnet should have been written by a Dominican monk in a Neapolitan prison in the first half of the seventeenth century, is truly note-worthy. It expresses the essence of democracy in a critique of the then existing social order.

XXVI. A very obscure piece of writing. The first quatrain lays down the principle that ill-doing brings its own inevitable punishment. The second distinguishes between the unblessed suffering which plagues the soul, and that which we welcome as a process of purgation. The first terzet makes heaven and hell respectively consist of a clean and a burdened conscience. The second, referring to a legend of S. Peter's controversy with Simon Magus, finds a proof of immortality in this condition of conscience.

XXVII. A bold and perilous image of the Machiavellian Prince, who drains the commonwealth for his own selfish pleasures. The play upon the words mentola and mente in the first line is hardly capable of reproduction.

XXVIII. Adami says in a note: Questo sonetto è fatto perchè l'intendano pochi; nè io voglio dichiararlo. Under these circumstances it is dangerous to attempt an explanation. Yet something may be hazarded. Line 1: the lady is Italy. Line 3: the stranger races are Rome's vassals. Line 7: Dinah is again Italy(?). Line 8: Simeon and Levi are the Princes of Italy and the Papacy. Line 9: Jerusalem probably stands for Rome. Line 10: Nazareth is the Gospel of Christ, and Athens is philosophy. Here again Adami warns us: qui legit intelligat. Line 13: a critique of the ruinous policy of calling strangers in to interfere in Italian affairs.

XXIX. Line 2: Attila is meant. The Venetian Lagoons were the refuge of the last and best Italians of the Roman age, when the incursions of the barbarians destroyed the classical civility. Line 12: alludes to the fixity of the Venetian Constitution and the deliberate caution of Venetian policy.

XXX. The quatrains describe the old power of Genoa, who conquered Pisa, abased Venice, planted colonies in the East, and discovered America. Line 10: throws the blame of Genoese decrepitude upon the nobles.

XXXI. Campanella praises the Poles for their elective monarchy, but blames them for choosing the scions of royal houses, instead of seeking out the real kings of men, such as he described in No. XVI.

XXXII. A similar criticism of the Swiss, who played so important and yet so contemptible a part in the Italian wars of the sixteenth century. With the terzets compare No. XXV. Line 11: stands thus in the original—La croce bianca e'l prato si contende.

XXXIII. A clever adaptation of the parable of the Samaritan, conceived and executed in the spirit of a modern poet like A.H. Clough.

XXXIV. Line 4: the hypocritical priest makes profit by preaching for holiness what is really hurtful to the soul. Lines 5-11 contrast the acknowledged sinners with the covert and crafty pretenders to virtue. Line 8: I have ventured to correct the punctuation. D'Ancona reads:

E poco è il male in cui poco è l'inganno. Ti puoi guardar:

but I am not sure that I am justified in the sense I put upon the verb guardarsi.

XXXV. A similar arraignment of impostors, comparing perfidious priests with the foulest literary scoundrel of the age, Pietro Aretino. The first terzet in the original is obscure.

XXXVI. I do not understand the allusion in the last line. The whole sonnet is directed against hypocritical priests.

XXXVII., XXXVIII., XXXIX. A commentary on the first clauses of the Lord's Prayer. Campanella tells the Italians they have no right to call themselves men, the children of God in heaven, while they bow to tyrants worse than beasts, and believe the lying priests who call that adulation loyalty. If they free their souls from this vile servitude, they may then pray with hopeful heart for the coming upon earth of God's kingdom, which shall satisfy poets, philosophers, and prophets with more than they had dreamed. It will be noticed that the rhymes are carried from sonnet to sonnet; so that the three form one poem, described by Adami as sonetto trigemino. In XXXVII., 13, I have corrected cenno into senno. In XXXIX., 1, I have ventured to render con ogni istanza by with every hour that flies, though istanza is not istante.

XL., XLL, XLII. These three sonnets, though not linked by rhymes, form a series, predicting the speedy overthrow of tyrants, sophists, hypocrites—Campanella's natural enemies—and the coming of a better age for human society. They were probably written early, when his heart was still hot with the hopes of a new reign of right and reason, which even he might help to inaugurate. The eagle, bear, lion, crow, fox, wolf, etc., are the evil principalities and powers of earth. No. XL., line 9: the giants are, I think, those lawless, selfish, anti-social forces idealised by Machiavelli in his Principe, as Campanella read that treatise—the strong men and mighty ones of an impious and godless world. No. XLL, line 4: concerning Taida, Sinon, Giuda, ed Omero, Adami says: 'These are the four evangelists of the dark age of Abaddon.' Thais is a symbol of lechery; Sinon of fraud; Judas of treason; Homer of lying fiction. So at least I read the allegory. No. XLII., lines 9-14 are noticeable, since they set forth Campanella's philosophical or evangelical communism, for a detailed exposition of which see the Civitas Solis.

XLIII. Invited to write a comedy—and it will be here remembered that Giordano Bruno had composed Il Candelaio—Campanella replied with this impassioned outburst of belief in the approaching end of the world. It belongs probably to his early manhood.

XLIV., XLV. Adami heads these two sonnets with this title: Sopra i colori delle vesti. It is a fact that under the Spanish tyranny black clothes were almost universally adopted by the Italians, as may be seen in the picture galleries of Florence and Genoa. Campanella uses this fashion as a symbol of the internal gloom and melancholy in which the nation was sunk by vice upon the eve of the new age he confidently looked for.

XLVI. The year 1603, made up of centuries seven and nine and years three, was expected by the astrologers to bring a great mutation in the order of our planet. The celestial signs were supposed to reassume the position they had occupied at Christ's nativity. Campanella, who believed in astrology, looked forward with intense anxiety to this turning-point in modern history. It is clear from the termination of the sonnet that he wrote it some time before the great date; and we are hence perhaps justified in referring the rest of his prophetic poetry to the same early period of his career.

XLVII. Qui legit intelligat, says Adami. Line 7: refers to the outlying vassals of the Roman Empire, who destroyed it, ruled Rome, and afterwards fell under the yoke of the Roman See. Lines 9-14 are an invective against the Papacy.

XLVIII. A sonnet on his own prison. The prison or worse was the doom of all truth-seekers in Campanella's age.

XLIX. For the understanding of this strange composition Adami offers nothing more satisfactory than mira quante contraposizioni sono in questo sonetto. The contrast is maintained throughout between the philosopher in the freedom of his spirit and the same man in the limitations of his prisoned life. Line 12 I do not rightly understand. Line 14 refers to Paradise.

L. There is an allusion in this sonnet to an obscure passage in Campanella's life. It seems he was condemned to the galleys (see line 12); and this sentence was remitted on account of his real or feigned madness. We should infer from the poem itself that his madness was simulated; but Adami, who ought to have known the facts from his own lips, writes: quando bruciò il letto, e divenne pazzo o vero o finto. Line 12: I have translated l'astratto by the mystic; astratto is assorto, or lost in ecstatic contemplation.

LI. To this incomprehensible string of proverbs Adami adds, ironically perhaps: questo è assai noto ed arguto e vero. It is an answer to certain friends, officers and barons, who accused him of not being able to manage his affairs. He answers that they might as well bring the same accusation against Christ and all the sages. Line 3: I have ventured to read è for e as the only chance of getting a meaning. Line 8: seems to mean that he would not accept life and freedom at the price of concealing his opinions.

LII. The same theme is rehandled. Lines 1-4: Campanella argued that a man's mental life extends over all that he grasps of the world's history. Line 5: the Italian for mite is marmeggio, which means, I think, a cheese-worm. The eclipse of Campanella's sun is his imprisonment. Lines 7 and 8 I do not well understand in the Italian. Line 11: 'Ye build the tombs of the prophets and garnish the sepulchres of the righteous,' Lines 12-14: saints and sages are made perfect by suffering.

LIII. A singular argument concerning prayer. Campanella says it is impious to hope to change the order and facts of the world, arranged by God, except in the single category of time. He therefore thinks it lawful for him to ask, and for God to grant, a shortening of the season of his suffering. See the Canzone translated by me, forming Appendix I.

LIV. Another sonnet referring to his life in prison. He asks God how he can prosper if his friends all fail him for various reasons. Lines 9-11 refer to the visit of a foe in disguise who came to him in prison and promised him liberty, probably with a view to extracting from him admissions of state-treason or of heresy. See the Canzone translated in Appendix I. The last three lines seem to express his unalterable courage, and his readiness to act if only God will give him trustworthy instruments and fill him with His own spirit. The Dantesque language of the last line is almost incapable of reproduction:

Ch' io m' intuassi come tu t' immii.

LV. Campanella tells his friend that such trivial things as pastoral poems will not immortalise him. He bids him seek, not outside in worn out fictions, but within his own soul, for the spirit of true beauty, turn to God for praise, instead of to a human audience, and go with the tabula rasa of childlike intelligence into God's school of Nature. Compare Nos I., V.

LVI. Campanella recognised in Telesio the founder of the new philosophy, which discarded the ancients and the schoolmen. Line 3: the tyrant is Aristotle. Lines 5 and 6: Bombino and Montano are the poets. Lines 7-9: Cavalcante and Gaieta were disciples of the Cosentine Academy founded by Telesio. Line 9: our saint, la gran donna, is the new philosophy. Line 12: my tocsin, mia squilla, is a pun on Campanella's name.

LVII. Rudolph von Bunau set himself at the age of sixteen to philosophise, travelled with Adami, and with him visited Campanella in prison at Naples. Campanella cast his horoscope and predicted for him a splendid career, exhorting him to make war upon the pernicious school of philosophers, who encumbered the human reason with frauds and figments, and prevented the free growth of a better method.

LVIII. Adami, to whom we owe the first edition of these sonnets, visited Campanella in the Castle of S. Elmo, having wandered through many lands, like Diogenes, in search of a man. Line 5: this, says Adami, 'refers to a dream or vision of a sword, great and marvellous, with three triple joints, and arms, and other things, discovered by Tobia Adami, which the author interpreted by his primalities'—that is, I suppose, by the trinity of power, love, wisdom, mentioned in No. VII. Line 6: Abaddon is the opposite of Christ, the lord of the evil of the age. Cp. note to No. XLI.

LIX. This is in some respects the most sublime and most pathetic of Campanella's sonnets. He is the Prometheus (see last line of No. I.) who will not slay himself, because he cannot help men by his death, and because his belief in the permanency of sense and thought makes him fear lest he should carry his sufferings into another life. God's will with regard to him is hidden. He does not even know what sort of life he lived before he came into his present form of flesh. Philip, King of Spain, has increased the discomforts of his dungeon, but Philip can do nothing which God has not decreed, and God never by any possibility can err.

LX. Arguments from design make us infer an all wise, all good Maker of the world. The misery and violence and sin of animate beings make us infer an evil and ignorant Ruler of the world. But this discord between the Maker and Ruler of the world is only apparent, and the grounds of the contradiction will in due time be revealed. See No. XIII. and note.

APPENDIX I

I have translated one Canzone out of Campanella's collection, partly as a specimen of his style in this kind of composition, partly because it illustrates his personal history and throws light on many of the sonnets. It is the first of three prayers to God from his prison, entitled by Adami Orazioni tre in Salmodia Metafisicale congiunte insieme.

I.

Almighty God! what though the laws of Fate
Invincible, and this long misery,

Proving my prayers not merely spent in vain
But heard and granted crosswise, banish me
Far from Thy sight,—still humbly obstinate
I turn to Thee. No other hopes remain.
Were there another God with vows to gain,
To Him for succour I would surely go:
Nor could I be called impious, if I turned
In this great agony from one who spurned,
To one who bade me come and cured my woe.
Nay, Lord! I babble vainly. Help! I cry,
Before the temple where Thy reason burned,
Become a mosque of imbecility!

II.

Well know I that there are no words which can
Move Thee to favour him for whom Thy grace
Was not reserved from all eternity.
Repentance in Thy counsel finds no place:
Nor can the eloquence of mortal man
Bend Thee to mercy, when Thy sure decree
Hath stablished that this frame of mine should be
Rent by these pangs that flesh and spirit tire.
Nay if the whole world knows my martyrdom—
Heaven, earth, and all that in them have their home—
Why tell the tale to Thee, their Lord and Sire?
And if all change is death or some such state,
Thou deathless God, to whom for help I come,
How shall I make Thee change, to change my fate?

III.

Nathless for grace I once more sue to Thee,
Spurred on by anguish sore and deep distress:—
Yet have I neither art nor voice to plead
Before Thy judgment-seat of righteousness.
It is not faith, it is not charity,
Nor hope that fails me in my hour of need;
And if, as some men teach, the soul is freed
From sin and quickened to deserve Thy grace
By torments suffered on this earth below,
The Alps have neither ice, I ween, nor snow
To match my purity before Thy face!
For prisons fifty, tortures seven, twelve years
Of want and injury and woe—
These have I borne, and still I stand ringed round with fears.

IV.

We lay all wrapped with darkness: for some slept
The sleep of ignorance, and players played
Music to sweeten that vile sleep for gold:

While others waked, and hands of rapine laid
On honours, wealth, and blood; or sexless crept
Into the place of harlots, basely bold.—
I lit a light:—like swarming bees, behold!
Stripped of their sheltering gloom, on me
Sleepers and wakers rush to wreak their spite:
Their wounds, their brutal joys disturbed by light,
Their broken bestial sleep fill them with jealousy.—
Thus with the wolves the silly sheep agreed
Against the valiant dogs to fight;
Then fell the prey of their false friends' insatiate greed.

V.

Help, mighty Shepherd! Save Thy lamp, Thy hound,
From wolves that ravin and from thieves that prey!
Make known the whole truth to the witless crowd!
For if my light, my voice, are cast away—
If sinfulness in these Thy gifts be found—
The sun that rules in heaven is disallowed.
Thou knowest without wings I cannot fly:
Give me the wings of grace to speed my flight!
Mine eyes are always turned to greet Thy light:
Is it my crime if still it pass me by?
Thou didst free Bocca and Gilardo; these,
Worthless, are made the angels of Thy might.—
Hast Thou lost counsel? Shall Thine empire cease?

VI.

With Thee I speak: Lord, thou dost understand!
Nor mind I how mad tongues my life reprove.
Full well I know the world is 'neath Thine eye.
And to each part thereof belongs Thy love:
But for the general welfare wisely planned
The parts must suffer change;—they do not die,
For nature ebbs and flows eternally;—
But to such change we give the name of Death
Or Evil, whensoe'er we feel the strife
Which for the universe is joy and life,
Though for each part it seems mere lack of breath.—
So in my body every part I see
With lives and deaths alternate rife,
All tending to its vital unity.

VII.

Thus then the Universe grieves not, and I
Mid woes innumerable languish still
To cheer the whole and every happier part.—
Yet, if each part is suffered by Thy will
To call for aid—as Thou art God most High,

Who to all beings wilt Thy strength impart;
Who smoothest every change by secret art,
With fond care tempering the force of fate,
Necessity and concord, power and thought,
And love divine through all things subtly wrought—
I am persuaded, when I iterate
My prayers to Thee, some comfort I must find
For these pangs poison-fraught,
Or leave the sweet sharp lust of life behind.

VIII.

The Universe hath nought that changes not,
Nor in its change feels not the pangs of pain,
Nor prays not unto God to ease that woe.
Mid these are many who the grace obtain
Of aid from Thee:—thus Thou didst rule their lot:
And many who without Thy help must go.
How shall I tell toward whom Thy favours flow,
Seeing I sat not at Thy council-board?
One argument at least doth hearten me
To hope those prayers may not unanswered be,
Which reason and pure thoughts to me afford:
Since often, if not always, Thou dost will
In Thy deep wisdom, Lord,
Best laboured soil with fairest fruits to fill.

IX.

The tilth of this my field by plough and hoe
Yields me good hope—but more the fostering sun
Of Sense divine that quickens me within,
Whose rays those many minor stars outshone—
That it is destined in high heaven to show
Mercy, and grant my prayer; so I may win
The end Thy gifts betoken, enter in
The realm reserved for me from earliest time.
Christ prayed but 'If it may be,' knowing well
He might not shun that cup so terrible:
His angel answered, that the law sublime
Ordained his death. I prayed not thus, and mine—
Was mine then sent from Hell?—
Made answer diverse from that voice divine.

X.

Go song, go tell my Lord—'Lo! he who lies
Tortured in chains within a pit for Thee,
Cries, how can flight be free
Wingless?—Send Thy word down, or Thou
Show that fate's wheel turns not iniquity,
And that in heaven there is no lip that lies.'—

Yet, song, too boldly flies
Thy shaft; stay yet for this that follows now!

APPENDIX II.

The 'Rivista Europea' of June 1875 publishes an article by Signor V. de Tivoli concerning an inedited sonnet of Michael Angelo, which he deciphered from the Autograph, written upon the back of one of the original drawings in the Taylor Gallery at Oxford. This drawing formed part of the Ottley and Lawrence Collection. It represents horses in various attitudes, together with a skirmish between a mounted soldier and a group of men on foot. Signor de Tivoli not only prints the text with all its orthographical confusions, abbreviations, and alterations; but he also adds what he modestly terms a restoration of the sonnet. Of this restoration I have made the subjoined version in rhyme, though I frankly admit that the difficulties of the text, as given in the rough by Signor de Tivoli, seem to me insuperable, and that his readings, though ingenious, cannot in my opinion be accepted as absolutely certain. He himself describes the MS. as a palimpsest, deliberately defaced by Michael Angelo, from which the words originally written have to be recovered in many cases by a process of conjecture. That the style of the restoration is thoroughly Michael Angelesque, will be admitted by all students of Signor Guasti's edition. The only word I felt inclined to question, is donne in line 13, where I should have expected donna. But I am informed that about this word there is no doubt. The sonnet itself ranks among the less interesting and the least finished compositions of the poet's old age.

Thrice blest was I what time thy piercing dart
  I could withstand and conquer in days past:
  But now my breast with grief is overcast;
  Against my will I weep, and suffer smart.
And if those shafts, aimed with so fierce an art,
  The mark of my frail bosom over-passed,
  Now canst thou take revenge with blows at last
  From those fair eyes which must consume my heart.
O Love, how many a net, how many a snare
  Shuns through long years the bird by fate malign,
  Only at last to die more piteously!
Thus love hath let me run as free as air,
  Ladies, through many a year, to make me pine
  In sad old age, and a worse death to die.

APPENDIX III.

The following translations of a madrigal, a quatrain, and a stanza by Michael Angelo, may be worth insertion here for the additional light they throw upon some of the preceding sonnets—especially upon Sonnets I. and II. and Sonnets LXV.-LXXVII. In my version of the stanza I have followed Michelangelo the younger's readings.

DIALOGUE OF FLORENCE AND HER EXILES.

Per molti, donna.

'Lady, for joy of lovers numberless

Thou wast created fair as angels are.
Sure God hath fallen asleep in heaven afar,
When one man calls the bliss of many his!
Give back to streaming eyes
The daylight of thy face that seems to shun
Those who must live defrauded of their bliss!'
'Vex not your pure desire with tears and sighs:
For he who robs you of my light, hath none.
Dwelling in fear, sin hath no happiness;
Since amid those who love, their joy is less,
Whose great desire great plenty still curtails,
Than theirs who, poor, have hope that never fails.'

THE SPEECH OF NIGHT.

Caro m' è'l sonno.

Sweet is my sleep, but more to be mere stone,
So lǒng as ruin and dishonour reign;
To bear nought, to feel nought, is my great gain;
Then wake me not, speak in an undertone!

LAMENT FOR LIFE WASTED.

Ohimè, ohimè!

Ah me! Ah me! whene'er I think
Of my past years, I find that none
Among those many years, alas, was mine;
False hopes and longings vain have made me pine,
With tears, sighs, passions, fires, upon life's brink.
Of mortal loves I have known every one.
Full well I feel it now; lost and undone,
From truth and goodness banished far away,
I dwindle day by day.
Longer the shade, more short the sunbeams grow;
While I am near to falling, faint and low.

Made in the USA
Las Vegas, NV
29 August 2023

76793532R00056